The Meat-Lover's Vegetarian Cookbook

Steven Ferry
and
Tanya Petrovna

JAIN PUBLISHING COMPANY
Fremont, California

Library of Congress Cataloging-in-Publication Data

Ferry, Steven, 1953—
    The meat lover's vegetarian cookbook / Steven Ferry and Tanya
Petrovna.
        p.   cm.
    ISBN 0-87573-070-1 (pbk. : alk. paper)
    1. Meat substitutes.   2. Cookery (Soybeans)   I. Petrovna, Tanya,
    1960—   . II. Title.
    TX838.F47   1997
    641.6'5655—DC20   96-42379
                                                                            CIP

Contents

List of Recipes

CHAPTER THREE - Making Meat and Other Animal Products!

CHAPTER FOUR - Classic American

CHAPTER FIVE - South of the Border

CHAPTER SIX - Those Familiar Italian Flavors

CHAPTER SEVEN - Chinese and Other Far East Feasts

CHAPTER EIGHT - Some Traditional European Cuisine

CHAPTER NINE - Breaking the Fast

CHAPTER TEN - Just Desserts

Fore or Five Words

A LITTLE PIECE OF PHILOSOPHY FROM A THIRD GENERATION CATTLE RANCHER

I was raised on a small, organic dairy farm in Montana during World War II. My parents milked the cows and left my grandparents to raise the children. Day care was different in those days: there were no swings, slides and lego blocks to play with. Instead, we worked full time in the garden and that's where my love of farming began: I knew I wanted to be a farmer.

This early decision made my approach to schooling very easy: I wanted to be a farmer and my parents owned a farm. There was therefore no need to pay any attention to the teachers because when school was over, I could start my career. All I did in the first twelve years at school was party and play football, both of which I was very good at. I have to admit that I was surprised when I graduated. The way I figured it later, the teachers must have thought I would be back if they didn't graduate me and that idea did not appeal to them. Whether I had a diploma or not, I was thrilled at the thought of becoming a farmer at last.

My first wake-up call came when I realized that farming was a business and that I lacked the tools to run one. Unwilling to let this dissuade me, I did what most American youth do when they have neglected to learn anything in the first twelve years of school—I enrolled in college.

I avoided the same mistakes I had made at high school and actually studied. I wanted to make our small organic dairy farm into an agribusiness, so I learned everything there was to know about herbicides, pesticides, hormones and medication. I graduated with a degree in agriculture from Montana State University with enough chemistry to qualify for a Nobel prize. I was finally certain I had the tools to succeed in my lifelong dream.

After twenty five years of hard work, I took that small organic dairy farm and turned it into an operation of one thousand range cows and calves, a five-thousand head confinement feedlot and thousands of acres of field crops. With up to thirty employees, I thought I was the Donald Trump of agriculture. No problem was too tough for me. If greater yields were needed, I used more herbicides. If insects were a problem, I used more pesticides. If more land or larger equipment was called for, I would buy out my neighbors, remove the fences and farm on a larger scale. I had all the answers.

That is, until I ended up in hospital in 1979, paralyzed from the waist down. My second wake-up call had arrived. The doctors thought a tumor was pressing on my spinal chord; they said if it was pressing on the inside of the chord, my chances of walking again were one-in-a-million. With those kind of odds being quoted, I knew I was being told to thumb through a catalog and pick out a wheelchair.

In that kind of situation, one is apt to wonder where one has gone wrong; the night before the operation, many ideas went through my mind, the most persistent of which was the picture of the soil I remembered from my childhood. After twenty-five years of chemical addiction, I had turned that living soil into matter that resembled asbestos; it looked like we had imported it from Mars. I knew I was responsible for the change and I couldn't blame anyone else.

I decided then that if I made it through the operation, I would do whatever I could to pass on our natural resources to the next generation. I wasn't sure what that meant except perhaps less use of chemicals, more crop rotation and a return to an organic form of farming.

The operation took twelve hours and the doctor's worst fears were realized. The tumor was not only inside the spinal chord but under it as well. Despite this, I was that one-in-a-million lucky trooper because I walked out of that hospital three weeks later.

It seemed to me on reflection that my childhood and university education had led me down the wrong path, so my first action was to re-educate myself. Like everyone else, I was brought up to believe that eating animal products was absolutely necessary for normal growth. I was told that milk was nature's most perfect food. Yet when I approached these ideas analytically, I was shocked by the amount of information that disputed them.

When I also traveled around the country, I found a whole generation of university-trained farmers such as myself had become chemical junkies, creating a whole new level of environmental problems. We had all been taken in by the advertising and public relations campaigns of the various industries involved in food production, whose chief concern was not with the health of the consumer, sustainable farming or the environment, but increasing their own sales.

As a first step after completing my tour of the country, I decided to at least turn my farm into an organic one; my farmer friends said the surgeons must have removed my brains along with the tumor. I talked to my banker about going organic and he reminded me that he was also the banker for the chemical and pharmaceutical dealers in town. If he helped me go organic, then their business would suffer from my loss of spending. Without any bank assistance, I could not support the debts I was carrying with the change to organic farming and was forced to sell most of my farm in 1983.

I then spent several years working with farmers and ranchers on the mounting problems associated with nonsustainable agriculture and by 1987, found myself working as a lobbyist for farmers on Capitol Hill. In the five years I worked with Congress, I learned the Golden Rule: Those that have the gold make the rules. When I am asked if all members of Congress are in the back pockets of special interests, I reply, "Not all, but almost all chairmen or subcommittee chairmen are totally beholden to big-money interests."

Rather than work through that pretense, I left Washington DC in 1992 and set up my own organization to educate Americans on the dangers of our diet and farming practices. As a farmer, I had almost killed myself with my diet while encouraging others to make the same mistake. It took a serious operation to make me face up to the facts about the way I was eating, and my misuse of animals and the land. It was hard to admit that my lifestyle had been wrong for years and even harder to tell my family and friends who still believed in that lifestyle.

Of the many interconnected problems in the environment, the most significant is man's consumption of animal products which result in mountains of animal manure, polluted water, overgrazing, rain forest destruction, soil loss and global warming, as well as human ill-health and hunger, and animal suffering. Time-wasting debates can be continued for as long as money exists to buy phony studies that cloud the issue, but the facts remain: We cannot survive on this planet with our present numbers if we continue to consume current quantities of animal products.

It would seem that the most dangerous weapon in the arsenal of the human race today is the table fork. It is hard to accept this when we sit in the tranquillity of our homes doing nothing more than eating. But my years of experience as a farmer, the thousands of people I have talked to, the mountains of research I have poured through, all indicate that the prescription for the health of all is an organic, plant-based diet. I have certainly changed mine, and hope that I can persuade you to at least try and do the same.

The Meat-Lover's Vegetarian Cookbook could not have come at a better time, because it provides recipes and a way of cooking that is as close as anyone can ever get to making dishes that we are all used to, but without using any animal products whatsoever. However much do-gooders say one should switch to a healthier diet for the sake of one's personal health or that of the environment, there's no way it'll happen if it costs too much or if it means foregoing the pleasures of eating the foods we like. Steven and Tanya have come up with a solution to these problems in putting together what I consider the best approach to introducing mainstream, meat-eating America to a plant-based diet; I hope you enjoy the vegetarian fare as much as I do.

Howard Lyman
Executive Director
Voice for a Viable Future

Introduction

Maybe it's news to you that the types of food health care professionals recommend we eat, as of the 8th of April 1991, no longer include meat, fish, and poultry. As if this isn't enough bad news, milk, eggs, cream and cheeses are also off-limits. With one announcement, the Physicians Committee for Responsible Medicine (PCRM), who made the recommendations, have jettisoned the meals and foods we have grown up with. Without any acceptable alternative, they expect us to kiss goodbye to hundreds of delicious dishes that thousands of chefs from many different countries have taken centuries to develop in response to our voracious appetites. At a time when almost every American can afford whatever his or her taste buds crave, from the typically American to the exotically foreign, just when it looks like we can have it all, some scrooge is saying, "No!"

The kicker is that the US Department of Agriculture (with a little prodding from the beef and dairy lobbies) told us the exact opposite nearly forty years ago when they introduced the original four food groups. At that time we were repeatedly admonished to grow big and strong with all the meat, fish, poultry, eggs and milk we could cram down our throats.

So what prompted the change? Our health did. We began to sicken and drop dead at a spectacular rate from degenerative diseases. Study after study and streams of statistics finally prompted the health industry to send out a clear message to its future patients: if you would like a slow and early death from cancer, heart attacks, and strokes; if you like being overweight and look forward to diabetes and degenerative diseases such as osteoporosis, then go ahead and continue eating dairy products, meats, fish and fowl, especially the ones that have been fed antibiotics and steroids and are even sometimes packaged up with their own excrement for your dining pleasure. Three out of every four deaths in America today result from degenerative diseases caused by the diet you and I eat.

> **Nothing will benefit human health and increase the chances of survival on Earth as much as the evolution to a vegetarian diet.**
>
> **—Albert Einstein**

The whole subject has been flogged to death. All we want to do is enjoy our meals without being lectured and made guilty; and later in our lives, keeling over from some horrible condition like Jacob Kreuzfeld disease (the human form of "mad cow disease" that is the beef industry's worst kept secret). How on earth did we get into such a mess? After all, we thought we were doing the right thing, eating all those protein-rich, Model T steaks and drinking that healthy milk.

It's ironic in the extreme that we have been persuaded to eat meat and dairy products, become hooked on them, dropping like flies as a result, and then been told we have been goofing up on our diet.

> **Every 45 seconds, someone dies of a heart attack in America. Those meat-eating males amongst us have a 50% chance of going this way. If we were to follow the new guide-lines, the chances reduce to 4%.**

Our diet kills a far greater proportion of Americans than do illicit drugs. Imagine the government in the 1950's, therefore, encouraging the use of street drugs, instead of meat and dairy products, as statistically less destructive. The media would have carried statements like:

"A Joint a Day Helps You Work, Rest and Play."

"Government reports indicate that your full nutritional needs can best be met by 1-2 snorts of coke a day."

That's stupid, obviously. But let's imagine on the other hand that the government at that time fully appreciated the dangers of meat and dairy consumption and took steps to protect the population from those dangers to its health and finances. The following might have been read in the papers:

"The government reports that 2 million people died needlessly of clogged arteries this year. A new bill is being rushed through Congress to crack down on illicit beef in the country."

"The Surgeon General, recently appointed as Food Czar, stated that interdictions of beef shipments from South America were up 50% this past quarter due to the deployment of military units along the border."

As absurd as the above scenarios are, they are no less off-the-wall than the government hooking all of us on food that is slowly killing us while choking the economy with health bills run amok.

In 1991, the four food groups we should be eating were re-defined as grains, legumes (i.e., beans and peas), vegetables, and fruit. This diet is high in fiber and nutrients. It is low in saturated and other fats and cholesterol. It is a diet that our grandparents and centuries of ancestors would recognize and is represented by the vegan diet today. Vegetarianism follows the same groupings but includes dairy products.

The likes of Thomas Edison, Albert Einstein and Benjamin Franklin were vegetarians, so it seems unlikely such a diet would shrink those little grey brain cells. As for meat being the food of athletes, Captain Jones of the USMC, a vegetarian, might have something to say about that: he holds the world record for consecutive sit-ups—17,003! And David Scott, another vegetarian, has won the Ironman Triathlon SIX times. These men are just two among many vegetarian athletes who excel. Could it be that we've all been fed a load of baloney about needing to eat meat in order to be strong? Who would want us to think such a thing?

> **One of the greatest armies in the world was vegetarian to a man: the Roman army conquered the known world on a diet of corn and barley. Caesar actually complained once that their supplies had run out and they had been forced to eat meat.**

The change in recommended diet by the PCRM received enough publicity at the time that most Americans were made aware of it, whether they agreed with it or not. For some, there is no alternative, as their degenerative conditions have become so advanced that their doctors insist on the change. But for the rest of us, we do have a choice at the moment; and while some have taken the plunge, most continue to enjoy their usual diets.

Bitter as the pill has been to swallow, though, there's even more to the message: If we want to enjoy the second half of our lives without these degenerative diseases, we also have to avoid excess sugar, salt, and processed foods. The majority of the food we eat is saturated in either salt or sugar; is liberally sprinkled with pesticides, herbicides, hormones, chemical additives and synthetic fertilizers; and has had most if not all the nutrients removed. It may taste good, the medics say, but as a source of energy to run the body, it is deceptive. It seems to fill us up, if we eat enough of it (which we do), but it undermines the cells, clogs up passages, overtaxes the organs, and usually by the fourth decade, starts to cause some major system-malfunctions. Then we pile on the drugs to mask the symptoms and start decorating the operating tables and paying the medicos' golf-club fees. After a few decades of this stop-and-go existence we dump our carcasses six feet under and call it quits.

> **The average age [longevity] of a meat eater is 63. I am on the verge of 85 and still work as hard as ever. I have lived quite long enough and am trying to die; but I simply cannot do it. A single beef-steak would finish me, but I cannot bring myself to swallow it. I am oppressed with the dread of living forever. That is the only disadvantage to vegetarianism.**
> **—George Bernard Shaw**

If this is where our current diet leads us, then we have two choices: to go for the same diet and suffer the consequences; or respond to medical advice and make the shift as smooth and gradual as possible.

Assuming you count yourself among those who view the promise of pain and disease as a good enough reason take evasive action, then your nose would seem to be pointing in the general direction of what? . . . vegetarianism! For most of us, that means rabbit food and hippies. As if the implied loss of the cowboy culture were not enough to deal with emotionally, do we now have to throw beads around our collective neck and start chewing alfalfa like the cows we prefer to eat?

Unfortunately, the vegetarian food we are being steered in the direction of eating has become synonymous with tasteless and boring dishes. The meals seem to be a collection of side orders on a plate: vegetables, grains or beans. Where's the meat! We need to have that savory taste and chewy or crisp texture we are used to, or the meal is not complete.

In fact, vegetarian cuisine has developed greatly over the last decade and many very tasty dishes do exist. Even when vegetarian dishes are well prepared, however, the craving for the old tastes and textures are not always satisfied. There are almost two hundred vegetarian cook books in print, and every single one of them addresses the twelve million vegetarians in the country. None deal with the key concerns the rest of us have about our eating pleasures. As a result, no acceptable cuisine has been provided that we can use. So we are damned if we do and damned if we don't as far as changing our eating habits is concerned.

The statistics speak for themselves. Only 5 in every 100 Americans are convinced enough to be vegetarians and even most of them eat dairy products. But there are promising signs of change in mainstream America. In the last few years, the number of people eating out at restaurants who ask for vegetarian dishes has jumped to 20 in every 100. And the estimated number of vegetarians has risen over 25% in the last five years, from 9 million to 12.5 million. So the health message is making in-roads. But what about the rest of us? Four in every five Americans still aren't willing to compromise taste today for better health tomorrow, even when the food is professionally prepared. And who can blame us? It's our choice, and both choices are pretty unpalatable. Can't we find some way of having and eating that juicy steak and cream-laden chocolate gateau and still living happily into our eighties?

The old adage that where there is an unresolving problem, one or both sides of the issue are based on incorrect information is certainly true in this quandary. It is not true that all vegetarian cooking is nothing but bland and boring steamed vegetables and rice. It doesn't take much to make it as tasty and interesting as meat-based diets. The idea that only meat can produce meat tastes is not correct. The idea that eggs and cream and cheeses are required to make creamy, rich sauces and desserts is not true. They can also be made using nuts and soy-based products. The cuisines we enjoy today have had hundreds of years to develop. Modern vegetarian cuisine as we know it has really only had a decade or two of attention from a handful of chefs. So there is much potential in the years ahead for developing the wide range of dishes we are used to. Twenty years ago, vegetarianism was just beans, grains and vegetables; none of the meat and dairy substitutes and recipes existed, except for some basic derivatives of the soy bean. Vegetarianism has come a long way since then and is ready to go mainstream now.

This cook book has been written to bridge the gap between what we eat and what we should be eating. It is written for the ninety-five percent of Americans who have been told they should be eating from the four new food groups, but neither like nor want to.

We want your taste buds titillated without risk to your future health. The hope is that *The Meat-Lover's Vegetarian Cookbook* will provide the yeast that will raise vegetarian cuisine into a recognizable shape, texture and taste for the majority of Americans. *The Meat-Lover's Vegetarian Cookbook* doesn't promise to make a shift to the recommended food groups that is completely unnoticeable. But it is the first cook book that is devoted solely to this issue with you in mind, and we have brought together everything we know to make it work for you.

CHAPTER ONE

How It Is NOT Done,
And How It IS Done

Before discussing the mechanical aspects of this cuisine, it is worth nuking a few sacred cows that exist for many of us about diet and food. With the wrong attitude, it's going to be hard for anyone to have fun with this or any other foods.

Number One, contrary to what you may have been told, we are not what we eat. If we were, we'd be eating ourselves. But we aren't, so therefore we aren't (what we eat). Now that we have that straight, it might help to know that I am me, and you aren't: you are you. We each have various reasons for stuffing food into our faces beyond feeding our bodies so they will last another day. We eat because it's time to eat, or because we are hungry. Or we drown our worries and sorrows. We eat because we like the taste of food or because we want to grow up or out. But anyone who thinks "I am what I eat" has done too much thinking for his or her own good. What the expression really means is: our bodies respond according to their ability to deal with the food we chuck into them. Eating junk food, for instance, eventually results in a junk body. There's no big mystery to that. Like everything else, what we put into something affects what we get out: therefore, what we eat influences the shape and condition of our bodies. So forget the mystical mumbo-jumbo.

Number Two, the fixation our culture has with food, diet and health is old; it's boring. We are better off knowing which foods have what effects on bodies, ours in particular; eating the foods that create the desired effect whenever possible; eating only when we are hungry; and insisting that the food tastes good and is enjoyable. And leaving the whole subject at that. Real sickness is worrying about calories and diseases and eating only the right foods in the right way. Phobias and aggravation take the pleasure away from eating and impair digestion.

7

Number Three, take with a pinch of salt every word the authors and anyone else says about what should or shouldn't be eaten. Blind faith and fear of claimed consequences violate Number Two above, resulting in fixations against which we feel obliged to waste further time and energy by rebelling and bingeing. It's better if we all make up our own minds based on what we find to be true regarding what we see, hear and are told. If we know enough people who have keeled over and died after numerous operations, and Dr. Cholesterol says it's because they ate too many burgers and chitlins, then maybe he has a point, and maybe he doesn't. It's our life and our call. We just shouldn't winge if we make the wrong one or if Medicare and Medicaid don't continue to pick up the tab.

If there is any broad statement the authors hold to be true, it is that the closer we eat to raw, unprocessed, and uncooked foods, the higher octane the fuel we supply our bodies so they will run efficiently and properly. With our sophisticated palates, we prefer creamier and more savory textures and tastes than are found in nature. Eating thus becomes a matter of balancing the body's need for nutrients with our desire for pleasurable eating.

Put another way, just because we put food in our mouths does not mean we are feeding our bodies what they need to run properly. Food has a certain shape, texture and taste, all of which we can perceive. But it also has something else that we cannot perceive so easily: nutrients, which the medicos call vitamins, minerals, enzymes, amino acids and so on. These all have one or more uses for the body. Trying to run a body without them is like trying to run a car without lubrication: after a while something seizes up and needs expensive repair.

When we eat food that has been processed (cut up, pieces removed, pasteurized, soaked and so on), some of these nutrients disappear. When food is then cooked, more nutrients are lost. Eating is a compromise because no-one wants, or is able, to eat a raw potato or chew through a bag of uncooked beans or grains. When we decide what to eat in any one meal or day, there is this balance to keep in mind and there are degrees of processing and cooking to choose from.

By insisting on food grown without chemical fertilizers, pesticides, herbicides or insecticides wherever possible; by using basic, raw ingredients and doing our own cooking, the nutrients reappear in our food and it tastes like grandma's home cooking. Steve's blue-blooded, meat-eating grandma's jaw dropped to the floor in amazement when she realized that she had grown up eating organic foods "just like the hippies do now." Needless to say, she remembered the food used to taste and smell right in those days—tomatoes smelled wonderfully of tomato and had a delicious tomato taste.

The way our bodies feel about processed foods is the same way we would feel (presumably) if someone gave us a large container and said, "Happy Birthday, here's a million bucks, spend it on whatever you want." As we feverishly open the lid, we find 50,000 $20 bills; but they've been run through a shredder and are lying in 2 inches of water, like so much papier mache. No-one can argue that there's one million dollars in the container, but how useful is it?

The Secret

Now that our heads are straight, let's get to our taste buds. So what's the secret? How do we get soggy noodles and limp broccoli to taste like a prime rib? How do we make a meal taste interesting without using gallons of oil and bushels of salt and sugar? Well, let's back up a bit and analyze what makes a meal tasty, and in particular, what qualities we look for when we eat meat and dairy products.

When we say food tastes good to us and we want more of it, there are actually five different factors a chef juggles to produce the exact right flavor. These are: sweet, sour, salt, bitter and spicy. In this cuisine, we make use of the following to achieve these flavors:

Sweetness is provided by fruits and most root vegetables, by most grains, and sweeteners such as maple syrup.

Sour is created by such as lemons, limes, cranberries, gooseberries, vinegars, wines (alcohol burns off in cooking), and pickled foods. These all have "pucker power."

Salt is provided by sea salt and items pickled or steeped in salt solution.

Bitter is produced by a few vegetables like chicory, watercress, mustard greens; as well as tea, coffee and red wines.

Spicy comes from condiments and spicey foods such as green onions, garlic, ginger, mustard, horseradish and chiles.

Many food manufacturers and restaurants rely on added sweeteners, salt, and oils to pep up food that has been made tasteless by overprocessing and overcooking. Because this book uses fresh ingredients and juggles all five factors of taste intelligently, the natural sweetness and flavors are enticed out of the food with a minimum of added sweeteners, salt, and fats.

As meat's taste comes from its amino acids, which vegetables, grains and legumes also have, it is not too hard to come up with meals that have the taste of meat that we are used to, especially when spices are added to mimic that savory kick we associate with animal products. In truth, meat on its own is bland tasting, which is why cuisines have developed different sauces and techniques over the years to spice them up.

The harder part has been to simulate meat textures. For this, we use the whole range of substitutes. The trick is first of all to use properly made and prepared substitutes. And then to use the right substitute for each particular application. Tofu (a soy bean derivative) is more like custard than meat and will not stand in for a steak. Seitan can on the other hand, being made of a firm wheat gluten. Ground beef is best simulated by TVP (Textured Vegetable Protein, another soy derivative). Fish is best simulated by Yuba (a soy derivative) but it's very hard to find. Tempeh (made from soy beans and rice or grains) is very good for hamburgers, although there are other equally good burgers on the market made with grains or vegetables, etc.

New products are constantly coming on the market to cater to the growing interest in vegetarian eating, and the result is vastly superior to the rubbery, hard-to-digest and poor tasting soy-based meat alternatives that were standard fare as little as ten years ago.

Henry Ford didn't just build cars; he was also a pioneer researcher into the soy bean and its uses. The first plastic car was developed as a result of Henry's knowledge of soy products. Later on, Avantis and Corvettes were made from synthetic plastics based on his developments. Henry Ford's leading research chemist worked for a company called Swift after Ford died and developed "bacon bits," which is a soy product (TVP).

We use bean, rice, or nut-based milks in place of animal milk for dairy products. Cheeses made from these products have been improving through the years and some are quite passable; in a couple of cases, they are indistinguishable from the real thing. It is worth checking the labels, though, because some are made with casein and calcium caseinate, both of them cow-milk derivatives; in which case you may as well eat the real thing. Sharon's Finest (800-656-9669) produces a completely vegan range of cheeses made of Brazil nuts and called Vegan Rella™. They have an interesting and pleasant taste and texture.

For those who want the exact flavors and textures of dairy cheeses, we suggest small quantities of the real thing be added almost as condiments. However, know that milk products in America are given the benefit of chemicals and hormones like no other country's, so you are better off purchasing organically produced milks and cheeses, or buying European cheeses where available. That is, of course, unless you do not mind being part of a poorly supervised experiment on the effect to your health of eating hundreds of chemicals and additives that have never existed before in your body.

Oils, tofu or nuts work very well as bases for cream substitutes.

For fats, we use olive and canola and a few other oils that are high in unsaturated fats and low in saturated fats. We also use amazake, which is creamy without being fatty, being a fermentation of cooked grains. We are not shy of using oils in some recipes, based on the understanding that the amount of oil actually consumed on this diet by each individual during the average day still falls within recommended limits.

Cold turkey vegetarianism for family and guests can be hazardous to your health.

As with most modern recipes, we have our eye on easily produced, quickly prepared meals, but there is only so much one can do to cut corners before the quality of the food suffers. If you are in a rush, throw in a microwave meal. But if you want a special meal it will take a wee bit of time and effort. These recipes take more than five minutes to put together; but by refrigerating or freezing leftovers and having the basic ingredients and basic foods (such as rice, beans, stocks, etc.) ready made in the refrigerator or freezer, you will be able to combine these with condiments and sauces and create that insta-meal when needed.

These recipes are low in cost at the grocery store and will save on the hospital bills in later years. We have tried wherever possible to use ingredients that can be found in most grocery stores. If you cannot find the ingredients there, ask the store manager to stock the items you want. Or go to a local health food store and have them special order if they don't have certain products. Or use the mail-order sources given in Chapter Three.

Even one meal a week from the four new food groups would be an improvement, so don't force the pace on yourself or family. Cold turkey is no fun.

> **Reducing meat and dairy consumption by 50% will reduce the risk of premature death from heart attack to 25%, from 50%. That means if four men were lined up in front of a firing squad, three of them would survive, rather than only two. Of course, if all four skipped meat and dairy products there wouldn't be any firing squad to worry about.**

If nothing else, badger the managers at the restaurants you go to: demand they buy this book and include some of the dishes on their menu. It'll be good business for them and most convenient for the rest of us.

We hope you will enjoy these recipes as much as we did in putting them together.

CHAPTER TWO

But Is It Appetizing?

Monotonous slop is a good description for the kind of institutional food we have probably all been glad to leave behind at some point in our lives. It is therefore worth looking over those points which make a meal or dish more appealing and which can help make a new cuisine more acceptable and pleasant.

Variety is the spice of life according to cuisine cliché, and there are various tools one can use to ensure those eating at ones table continue to do so.

People eat with their eyes, so don't rely on the lone garnish to add some pizzazz. Make the food on the plate as visually appealing as a painting: use the different colors and shapes of foods to attract the eye; make each element work together.

When someone bites into their food, they don't want a series of mushy textures. Vary the soft with the crunchy, the chewy with the crisp.

Menu planning for a week or a few days at a time will help create variety, so that burgers don't figure as the "piece de la resistance" of four meals in a row. And if you really only have a bag of rice in the family, at least you can make sure it is fried one day and boiled the next, and so on.

Variety can also be enhanced by taking a particular cuisine as a theme for a meal. Italian Night when there's romance in the air, American Night before the ball game, and so on.

Foods have aromas which can be played up as much as possible to make mouths water.

Use herbs and spices to enhance existing tastes. That means using only enough to create a more complex flavor; too much seasoning will drown the flavor of the original food. As long as dried herbs and spices are no older than six months, they are as flavorful as fresh ones; but they are three to four times stronger by volume, so substitute accordingly. Fresh herbs should be prepared and used toward the end of cooking so as to retain their flavor, while dried ones are better added early on. Whether dried or fresh, herbs should be added at the beginning in uncooked dishes so that the flavors blend and develop.

Salt may be anathema to some people, but dishes can generally stand a small amount to bring out flavors fully. Herbs, spices, garlic, peppers, mustard, ginger, horseradish, lemons and lime all help make up any short-fall experienced when salt is reduced in a diet.

> **Have you ever tried to fathom why some seasonings are called "spices" and others "herbs"? Spices come from the roots, seeds, dried berries and bark of plants in tropical and sub-tropical climate zones. Herbs come from the leaves of plants in temperate climate zones.**

Create and use different decorations for the table to suit the chosen cuisine; supplement with different decors or rooms to enhance the chosen ambience.

A note of caution when menu planning: avoid over-indulgence in meat substitutes. These are processed foods that are harder on the gut than fresh fruits, vegetables, whole grains, and legumes. A rough nutritional balance would be 40% grains, 40% fruits and vegetables, and 20% legumes, with a good proportion being unprocessed.

As a final note, we want this book to provide the basic tools for you to successfully adapt your favorite recipes, as well as cookbooks that you already have, to the new Vegetarian Meat Cuisine. So study how we do it and then start applying the principles yourself; there's plenty of room for innovation and creation in Vegetarian Meat Cuisine.

CHAPTER THREE

Making Meat And
Other Animal Products!

The simplicity of the idea is to make or buy basic meat and dairy substitutes and keep them in the fridge or pantry for use as recipes call for them. Recipe times are therefore cut way down and meals become easy to produce, sometimes even instant. This, together with simplified techniques, is how we cut corners with our recipes. Other advantages to using alternatives to animal products is that you don't have to worry about animal products going off or contaminating other foods or work surfaces. And you don't have to go shopping regularly to buy perishables.

Obviously, you will only make your own meat and dairy products if you have the time and inclination. If not, spend more money to buy the ready-made products (some products and sources are listed in this chapter). Some are excellent and some are good enough. Experiment to find the ones you like.

Meats

When you were growing up, you probably never thought you would be making the meat you eat; but make no bones about it, this chapter is leading you down the slippery path to fully fledged Meat-Maker. There are two parts to the process of making meat: having an almost tasteless product with some kind of chewy texture; and then marinating or stewing that product to imbue it with the various savory flavors we associate with animal flesh.

There are various types of meat that have been turned into delicacies through the ages, but only a handful of substitutes so far invented, most revolving round the sturdy soy bean. Our job of making authentic taste-alikes from these few substitutes has been made easy because most meats have no real flavor of their own. We have created four mild meat flavors by using different stocks in which to stew the meat substitutes. By then adding different sauces, a wide range of complex tastes can be created. Making stocks may seem like too much hard work, so they are only provided for those amongst us who realize that stocks really are easy to create while being the foundation of any professional kitchen. If you have neither the time nor inclination, then at least buy some (vegetarian) stocks and use them instead to flavor your meats.

Or better still, if you want an easy way to make a simply delicious, meaty and thick stock, then try this: save water from making pasta and use it to make beans which you then drain. And voilà, a delicious stock is made. The flavors vary according to the beans you use. You could equally well make beans and then pasta, it doesn't matter the order.

There are three key products we use as meat substitutes:

Seitan

Seitan is an ancient, oriental food made of wheat gluten. The gluten flour is mixed with water to form a lump of dough which is then simmered, fully submerged, in various stocks (traditionally Tamari soy sauce and spices are used) for four hours. Seitan can be bought ready-made in jars or boxes at greater cost of course. Some brands can be too salty, or rubbery in texture, so don't give up on seitan if you hit a rough brand at first. Seitan is low in calories, easy to digest for most people and has about 15 grams of protein in a 4-oz serving.

> **Seitan will keep in the refrigerator or freezer. If it comes out slightly spongy after being made, it can be diced and lightly fried in oil for half an hour to stiffen the outer layer, following the sausage recipe (p. 20).**

Textured Vegetable Protein

Otherwise known as "hydrologized vegetable protein" and "textured soy flour" on the labels of canned and packaged foods, TVP for short is made of soy flour that has had the soybean oil removed. TVP comes in anything from small granules to chunks and slices. It is bought dried and then reconstituted in boiling water or stock (about equal parts TVP to liquid) until double its size, and then added to dishes. It can also be added dry during the cooking process as long as there is as much liquid as TVP in the pot. TVP is loaded with protein and has almost no fat.

Worthington (800-628-3663) makes granulated TVP, and it can also be ordered from Harvest Direct (800-835-2867) and Heartline (800-256-2253). Harvest Direct and Heartline both have custom-made their products into textures and flavors that closely approximate beef, chicken and sausage, in granulated and sliced form.

Tempeh

Made from soybeans and grains such as millet, tempeh has been a staple in Indonesia for centuries. Like cheese, yoghurt, and sourdough, tempeh is made by natural culturing. The protein in tempeh is partially broken down during the fermentation process, making it highly digestible. Avoid buying or eating tempeh with red, green or yellow mould; a small amount of black or grey mould is edible and actually enhances the flavour. Tempeh should be firm but slightly pliable.

Basic tempeh on the market are not as appetizing as it could be. Adequate but heavy patties are made by White Wave (303-443-3917). The best we've ever had are made (not surprisingly) by Tanya who mail orders if you call 1-800-705-7115.

Now, to the actual recipes for the four stocks:

Beef

Make stock with the recipe below and then either use to reconstitute TVP products (sitting in boiled stock for 10 minutes); or use it to cook raw seitan for a few hours. If using tempeh, it can be marinated, pan-fried or otherwise cooked in the stock.

> **When boiling seitan in stock, the stock reduces and becomes concentrated. It should be saved and re-used but will need to have water added so as to maintain a light rather than an overly salty flavor.**

Beef Stock

20 cups water
2 cups shoyu soy sauce
1 onion, peeled and quartered
10 garlic cloves, peeled
1 3-inch piece of ginger, unpeeled, sliced
7 bay leaves

1. Combine ingredients, bring to boil and let cool.

> **Avoid the synthetic, supermarket soy sauces which have caramel, synthesized soy, corn syrup and sometimes MSG in them and which take only a few days to make. Instead, find the traditional brew of soy beans, salt and water which are allowed to ferment in wooden vats for a year or more. We prefer the wheat-free Tamari soy sauce (Shoyu soy sauce has wheat in it) because it has more amino acids and is fuller flavored. If fermented foods are a problem for anyone, try Bragg Liquid Aminos, also made from soy beans. It is not fermented, but has a fine, soy-like taste.**

One of the best beef textures is produced by Heartline—order their chunky chicken TVP, in preference to their beef fillet product, though. Or try Griddle Steaks (La Loma, Worthington Foods 800-628-3663) and Upcountry Seitan (413-298-3854).

Chicken, Turkey and Cornish Game Hen

This stock has a fowl taste, which serves well for chicken, turkey, cornish game hen, and even rabbit recipes.

Chicken Stock

20 *cups water*
4   *cups vegetarian chicken stock*

1. Heat water and mix in powder.

The best texture for birds is usually TVP chunks, although tempeh can work well and seitan works for larger pieces, such as turkey.

There are various makes of vegetarian chicken stock on the market, requiring differing ratios of powder to water. Use enough powder (or paste) to make a strongly flavored stock. One we recommend, if you are in California, is Vegetarian Style Chicken Broth by Ralphs Private Selection (they do not mail order).

Game Birds and Animals

Use the lamb recipe below, omitting $1/2$ teaspoon salt but adding 2 cups of soy sauce for that gamey flavor of venison, duck, pheasant, reindeer, moose and whatever other wild creatures we see fit to cut down, carve up and grace our dining tables with. Makes 10 cups.

Lamb Stock

For sweeter-tasting meats such as lamb, veal or pork, use the following stock which makes 8 cups:

4   *onions, sliced*
16 *garlic cloves, sliced*
2   *tablespoons sea salt*
12 *cups water*
4   *oz dried shiitake (or Morel) mushrooms*
$1/2$ *cup olive oil*
10 *celery stalks, sliced*
6   *carrots, sliced*
2   *leeks, sliced*
1   *teaspoon pepper*
4   *bay leaves*
1   *cup chopped parsley ($1/3$ cup dried)*

19

> 2   *tablespoons thyme (1 teaspoon dried)*
> 2   *teaspoons sage (³/₄ teaspoon dried)*

1. In a large pot with a heavy bottom, heat oil and sauté onions and garlic on medium high for 2 minutes, then on low until browned (about ¹/₂ an hour). Stir occasionally and after 15 minutes, add salt to release juices.

2. Meanwhile, reconstitute mushrooms in 4 cups hot water for ¹/₂ hour.

3. Agitate mushrooms in water to settle grit at bottom of bowl, place mushrooms aside, strain and reserve liquid.

4. To onions, add celery, carrots, leeks, seasoning, and cook 5 minutes.

5. Add remaining water, mushrooms and liquid, bring to boil and simmer 1 hour.

6. Strain stock and reduce as needed.

Ground Beef

TVP works best for this type of food—it's almost impossible to tell it from the real thing in dishes such as Sloppy Joe's. Ground TVP is available unflavored from Worthingtons or flavored from Heartline's.

Sausage

Makes 2 cups
10 minutes and 1 hour heating

> 2   *tablespoons olive oil*
> 6   *shallots, sliced*
> 6   *garlic cloves, sliced*
> 2   *cups (seitan) beef, ¹/₄-inch cubes*
> ¹/₂ *cup beef stock (p. 18)*
> ¹/₄ *teaspoon crushed red pepper*

1. Sauté shallots and garlic in oil 3 minutes, add the beef and sauté 2 more minutes.

2. Add beef stock and pepper, and leave on low about an hour, stirring occasionally until sausage somewhat crispy.

Burgers

You can make your own burgers by flavouring tempeh patties using our burger recipe (pg 39). This combination makes the best burgers in terms of taste and texture.

There are many pre-made and flavored burgers on the market utilizing tempeh, tofu, vegetables, rice and even wheat. They are listed so you can order them directly or via retail stores and determine which ones you like.

Turtle Island makes tempeh "superburgers" if you can find them. Island Spring, Inc. (206-463-9848) makes TofuBurgers in various flavors for the Northwest market. Mandarin Soyfoods (107-11031 Bridgeport Road, Richmond, BC Canada V6X 3A2) makes various flavors, including spicy cajun and BBQ, out of a soy, rice and vegetable mix. Sizzle Burgers (LaLoma, Worthington Foods) are made of soy and grains, but include egg whites.

Various other meats, ready made:

Links: Healthy Links by White Wave Soyfoods are well textured and spicy.

Franks and Dogs, various quite accessible on market, especially Natural Touch Vege Franks.

Corndogs: LaLoma by Worthington.

Pepperoni: Vegan Epicure (607-272-0432). Made of seitan, they have many other meats, using flavors from cuisines around the world.

Deli slices/cold cuts: Turkey, roast beef, corn beef, pastrami, ham, all by Heart and Soul (Legume Inc., phone 201-263-1013). And Yves Veggie Deli slices (Yves Veggie Cuisine, Inc, Vancouver, BC, Canada V6A 2A8).

Beef Jerky: Garden of Eatin (1-800-333-5244) and Heartline, who have several flavors.

> **The irony of the soybean is that although it originated in the Far East, America now produces more soybeans than all other countries combined and sends most of them, as its largest cash crop and agricultural export, to Asia. These Asian countries then make products out of these American-grown soybeans and export most of them back to America.**

Tofu

Notice that we do not recommend tofu as a meat look/taste-alike. Tofu is made by cooking soy milk and adding a natural solidifier which causes the curd to separate from the whey. The whey is drained off and the curd pressed into a block. Some tofu is soft and silky and is ideal for blending into a cream or paste. Other tofu is denser (has less water content) and is better for slicing, deep frying or crumbling. The packaging usually states extra firm, firm, soft or silken.

Quorn

Quorn is a trademark for a meat substitute made from a tiny relative of the mushroom that grows underground. It is commercially grown and then fermented. Egg white is added. Quorn is not superior to TVP chunks in texture, but it does offer a plant-based alternative to those wanting a change from TVP. It also compares very favourably with tofu, having less fat but more protein and fibre content. It is made by Marlow Foods, Ltd. (9 Station Road, Marlow, Buckinghamshire SL7 1NG, UK).

Fish

For white fish, try extra-firm tofu, sauteed in white wine. Probably the best fish rendition is Yuba, another soy product. It is very thin and can be oiled and layered much like filo pastry sheets and then either fried to produce a flaky texture or baked to give a crunchy and chewy one. The only problem is that unless you have access to an Asian market, you probably won't be able to find any, as we don't know anyone who mail orders the dried product.

Natural Touch Okara Patties by Worthington Foods work well for fish texture, even though they aren't marketed as a fish substitute. Or try Sea Veggie Tempeh by White Wave and cut to size of fillet desired.

Dairy Products

Now that we have dealt with meats, what about dairy products? Cheese alternatives exist made of soy, tofu and almonds. With the exception of a grated parmesan called "Lite 'N Less" (by Soyco Foods, 800-441-9419; or mail order from Harvest Direct, 800-835-2867), we haven't found any that are truly satisfactory. We've tried various ways of making cheese ourselves, without success to date. However, if you happen to be in Great Britain, one company (Bute Island Foods, Rothesay, Isle of Bute PA20 ODN; phone 0700-505117) makes a cheddar style "Scheese" from soy products which is superb, both in texture and tang. If you feel sufficiently inspired, they would like someone to manufacture and distribute the product in America. . . .

We won't bother you with all the nasty tales about what is in milk these days, but suffice to say, it's nothing your great grand-parents would recognize. If you have to eat cheese, do yourself a favor and find a local farm that produces organic cheese. Or go for goat cheese, which tends to be somewhat tangy. Otherwise, try the alterna-tives that have no casein in them. After a while, you'll get used to the slightly rubbery texture and only occasionally yearn for the real thing.

For **butter** in some savory contexts we recommend our **garlic butter recipe** as follows:

1. Preheat oven to 350° F, peel two cups of garlic cloves, place in a small baking dish and cover with extra virgin olive oil, about 1 cup.
2. Bake 30 – 40 minutes until golden.
3. Let cool, refrigerate and then blend with a food processor until emulsified.

4. Refrigerate and it can last several weeks, but in practice is usually used much faster. Apart from the many uses in the recipes of this book, garlic butter can be used

• to replace regular butter at the table

• as a spread on a toasted baguette that is also sprinkled with chopped, fresh parsley and finely grated parmesan for a delicious garlic bread

• to toss in pasta with parsley and parmesan as above, and freshly ground pepper added.

For frying, use the butter spray made by El Molino (Pearl River, New York 10965) or olive oil in the new pump-action spray bottles available in health food stores.

For **mayonaise**, there is an excellent product called Nayonaise® (available in most health food stores and supermarkets around the country, made by Nasoya, 800-229- 8638) which is made from soy and without eggs.

For **ice cream**, there are products on the market made of rice and soy. The best in our humble opinion (and those whom we've tested the various makes on) is Steven's own, made of nuts (pg 153). But if you don't have the time to make your own, then can we recommend Sweet Nothings (Turtle Mountain Inc., POB 70, Junction City, OR 97448, 503-998-6947). Theirs is not as rich and creamy as Steven's, but it has the added advantage of having no fat and cholesterol, whereas Steven's has some nut oils in it. Tofutti Brands (50 Jackson Drive, Cranford, NJ 07016, 908-272-2400) are also tasty and creamy, but have as much fat in them as most regular diet ice creams.

For **cream** in desserts, Steven's cream (p. 153) doesn't just lead the field, it IS the field, unless you prefer a long list of chemicals in your non-dairy creams.

For **chocolate**, try a tofu version, Tropical Source, available from mail order catalogs (800-669-8875 or 800-347-0070).

And for **milk**, there is a wide array of products on the market made of soy, almonds and rice. Like dairy milk, they vary in fat content and taste, but work well for cereals, cooking, and even drinking. Harvest Direct carries two types of milk (800-835-2867).

Without becoming paranoid over finding or making animal product substitutes, it is possible to stock a wide range of non-animal based meat and dairy products for use whenever needed. After the initial work of finding good sources and getting the hang of making the different stocks and meats is over, your shopping and cooking will simplify greatly.

NOW, THEN, HAPPY? WE DON'T LOVE YOU FOR YOUR BODY ANYMORE... BUT FOR YOURSELF!
FRAPAR.

CHAPTER FOUR

Classic American

Much of modern American food has been processed into tasteless-ness in order to preserve shelf life and then drowned in sugar and salt to make it palatable. But traditional dishes used to burst with flavor and can once again. This chapter reflects the many roots of American cuisine from French to Italian to African and so on.

SLOPPY JOE'S

Where would home cooking be without a steaming plate of Sloppy Joe's?

Serves 4 - 6
15 minutes preparation and 15 minutes sauteing

1 ½ cups (TVP) ground beef
1 ¼ cups beef stock (pg 18)
3   tablespoons olive oil
1   onion, finely chopped
2   cloves garlic, finely chopped
½   red bell pepper, finely chopped
1   28-oz can crushed tomatoes
1 ½ teaspoons sea salt
½   teaspoon pepper

1. Combine beef and stock in a pan, bring to boil and let sit 10 minutes.
2. In a sauté pan, heat olive oil. Add onions and garlic, sauté until transparent and lightly browned (about 2 minutes). Add bell pepper and sauté for another 2 minutes. Add ground beef, sauté for 3 – 4 minutes on medium low heat. Add crushed tomatoes, salt and pepper. Simmer for about 15 minutes on medium low heat.
3. Serve over your favorite toasted hamburger buns.

MEAT LOAF WITH GARLIC MASHED POTATOES

Serves 4-6

15 minutes plus 40 minutes baking

1 ¼ cups beef stock (pg 18)
1 ½ cups (TVP) ground beef
1   onion, finely chopped
2   tablespoons cup olive oil
1 ½ cups tomato sauce (pg 85)
3   oz tomato paste
2   teaspoons dried oregano
2   teaspoons dried thyme
1   cup lecithin granules*
½   pound firm tofu
3   cups bread, ¼-inch cubes

1. Heat stock and reconstitute beef in it for 10 minutes.

2. Sauté onions in oil until transparent and slightly browned, about 3 minutes. Add ground beef and sauté until brown, about 3 minutes.

3. Preheat oven to 375° F.

4. In a food processor or blender, puree tomato sauce and paste with tofu, oregano and thyme.

5. Combine all ingredients in a large bowl, pour into a lightly oiled loaf pan and cover.

6. Bake for 30 minutes. Remove cover and bake for an additional 10 minutes.

7. Serve with garlic mashed potatoes (recipe follows).

* Available in health food stores.

GARLIC MASHED POTATOES

Serves 4
20 minutes plus 30 minutes cooking/cooling

6   *medium potatoes, quartered**
1   *cup soy milk*
¹/₄ *cup coconut milk*
3   *tablespoons garlic butter (pg 23)*
1   *teaspoon salt*
¹/₂ *teaspoon pepper*

1. Boil water while peeling and quartering potatoes. Boil potatoes until fork tender, 10 – 15 minutes.
2. Combine all ingredients in a food processor and mash until smooth.

* We suggest using potatoes with a yellow finish, such as Yukon Gold.

One third of all raw materials consumed in America goes toward the raising of livestock.

SPAGHETTI WITH MEATBALLS

Serves 6
5 minutes plus 15 minutes

1   cup canola oil
1   pound (seitan) beef (pp 16 & 18), cubed
4   cups basic tomato sauce (pg 85)
1   pound spaghetti of your choice
     Grated (soy) Parmesan to taste (optional)

1. Cook spaghetti per package instructions.
2. Gently heat tomato sauce.
3. In heavy skillet, heat canola oil. Gently place meat balls in hot oil; cook until well browned, about 2 minutes.
4. Remove balls and drain on paper towel. Add to heated tomato sauce. Keep warm.
5. Pour tomato & meatball sauce over spaghetti; serve with Parmesan cheese (optional) and garlic bread (pg 23).

PEPPER STEAK

Chinese cuisine broadened the horizons of European cooks centuries ago. When the Chinese in turn were exposed to European and New World food items in modern times, they continued to create exciting new flavors. The pepper steak is one such dish that we owe the Chinese of modern times.

Serves 4
15 minutes

2	_tablespoons olive oil_
4	_(seitan) beef fillets, 1" thick (pg 16)_
5	_shallots, thinly sliced_
2	_tablespoons coarsely ground black pepper_
2	_tablespoons cognac (or whiskey)_
¹/₂	_cup beef stock (pg 18)_
1	_bunch of chives, finely chopped_

1. In a skillet or frying pan, heat olive oil and brown fillets on one side (2 – 3 minutes). After about one minute, add the shallots to the frying pan and allow to brown alongside fillets.

2. Turn fillets and press pepper corns firmly into top side while browning the other side.

3. Carefully pour stock and cognac over and around fillets.

4. Reduce liquid to thick, flavorful sauce, about 2 minutes.

5. Place fillets on serving plates and spoon sauce evenly over them. Garnish with chopped chives.

BEEF STEW

Serves 6
20 minutes and 30 minutes cooking

1   *lb (seitan) beef, ¹/₂-inch cubes (pp 16 & 18)*
2   *cups water*
1   *onion, sliced*
2   *cloves garlic, minced*
2   *bay leaves*
1   *tablespoon soy sauce*
¹/₂   *cup burgundy or similar red wine*
1   *tablespoon maple syrup*
¹/₄   *teaspoon pepper*
¹/₄   *teaspoon paprika*
    Pinch of allspice or cloves
1   *lb carrots, cubed*
1   *lb potatoes, cubed*
1   *lb small white onions*
    Wholewheat or unbleached Flour

1. Brown beef in skillet sprayed with oil while preparing vegetables and boiling water in a large pot.

2. Add remaining ingredients except flour to pot.

3. Simmer, covered, until vegetables tender, stirring occasionally and add water if needed.

4. Mix flour into paste with water and add to thicken.

5. Stir in beef.

JAMBALAYA

Jambalaya is a dish made of left overs and is popularly thought to mean "clean up the kitchen." The word itself comes from the French words for "ham" (jambon) and "with" (à la), followed by the African word "ya" for "rice."

Serves 6
25 minutes plus 2 hours baking

¹/₄	cup olive oil
1	medium onion, chopped
4	garlic cloves, chopped
1	cup peeled and chopped tomatoes
1	cup tomato sauce
1	cup chopped celery
1	cup chopped green bell pepper
1	teaspoon chopped parsley
2	tablespoons thyme (1 teaspoon dried)
1 ¹/₂	teaspoons sea salt
1 ¹/₂	teaspoons pepper
1	teaspoon cayenne
2	bay leaves
4	teaspoon dried sage
2	tablespoons of balsamic vinegar
2	cups long grain brown rice, rinsed
1	cup (TVP) beef chunks
6	cups beef stock (pg 18)
1	cup sausage, diced (pg 20)

1. Preheat oven to 350° F.
2. In large skillet, sauté onions and garlic in oil five minutes.
3. Stir in tomato and sauce and bring to simmer.
4. Stir in celery and bell pepper.
5. Stir in seasonings, vinegar, rice, beef chunks, stock and bring to boil.
6. Add sausage.
7. Place in casserole dish, cover with foil and bake 2 hours until rice is cooked.

Serve with cornbread and salad.

ROAST TURKEY AND CHESTNUT STUFFING

Serves 4
20 minutes

¼ cup olive oil
5 shallots, thinly sliced
5 cloves of garlic, thinly sliced
1 pound (seitan) turkey (pp 16 & 18), cut into ¼" thick slices
Salt
Black pepper

1. In a skillet, heat oil over medium heat. Sauté shallots and garlic until lightly browned and transparent, about 2 minutes.
2. Add turkey slices. Cover skillet and brown 3 – 4 minutes. Turn slices over and brown another 2 minutes. Reduce heat and cook another 4 minutes. Add salt and pepper to taste.
3. Serve with garlic mashed potatoes (pg 29), stuffing (see below) and cranberry sauce.

Chestnut Stuffing

Serves 4
10 minutes plus 45 minutes soaking/baking

1 cup peeled chestnuts
8 slices (stale) bread*
2 cups of (soy) milk
2 teaspoons dried oregano
1 teaspoon dried thyme
3 tablespoons vegetarian chicken-stock powder
½ teaspoon black pepper
½ cup chopped celery
½ onion, finely chopped

1. Preheat oven to 350° F.
2. Cut bread slices into ¼" cubes. Soak in soy milk for about 20 minutes.
3. Mix in remaining ingredients.
4. Lightly grease a baking dish, fill with bread mixture and bake at 350° F for 25 minutes.

* Preferably whole grain, but you can use the bread of your choice.

CHICKEN SOUP (or Pot Pie)

The original "soupes" were really no more than chunks of bread flavored with broth. While not as thick, this soup has plenty of chunks in it and makes a hearty meal in itself.

Serves 6
20 minutes (35 for pie) plus 1 ½ hours cooking

2	_tablespoons olive oil_
1	_spanish onion, coarsely chopped_
1	_bunch green onions, ¼-inch slices_
4	_cloves garlic, chopped coarsely_
1	_tablespoon salt_
¼	_cup whole wheat flour_
2	_quarts reconstituted vegetarian chicken broth_
1	_teaspoon pepper_
1	_tablespoon each of fresh, ground rosemary, tarragon, oregano_
2	_cups chicken (shredded seitan or TVP chunks) (pp 16 & 19)_
1	_tablespoon mustard_
1	_cup white wine_
1	_lemon, juiced_
6	_stalks celery, ¼-inch slices_
10	_carrots, ¼-inch slices_
5	_potatoes, peeled and cubed ¼-inch_

1. In large, heavy-bottomed soup pot, heat oil and sauté onions, green onions and garlic. After 5 minutes, add salt.

2. Sprinkle and stir in flour.

3. Add stock, bring to boil and simmer for few minutes, adding rest of ingredients.

4. Heat for 1 ½ hours at a low simmer until vegetables tender.

Variation

To make into a pie, use only one quart of chicken broth, reduce stewing to 1 hour and make a crust as follows:

1 ½	_cups unbleached white flour_
½	_cup whole wheat pastry flour_

$^1/_4$ *teaspoon sea salt*
$^1/_2$ *cup soy milk*
$^1/_3$ *cup canola oil*

1. Mix flours and salt.
2. Whisk oil into milk.
3. Add wet to dry ingredients and form into a ball.
4. Divide ball in half and roll out on floured surface.
5. Place chicken in a casserole dish, lay crust on top, and use any excess dough to decorate crust; make air holes in the crust.
6. Bake 30 minutes until crust lightly browned.
7. Let sit 15 minutes before serving.

CRAB CAKES WITH SHERRY SAUCE

We don't remember where we found this basic Dungeness crab recipe, but it has pleased diners over the years and is reportedly better than the crab cakes from The Four Seasons in New York, while being kinder on the arteries and wallet.

Serves 4
30 minutes plus 30 minutes refrigeration

_12_	_oz (tempeh) patties_
_1_	_packet kombu* (or salt if unavailable)_
_1 ³/₄_	_cups dry bread crumbs_
_1_	_celery rib, minced_
_2_	_scallions, minced_
_¹/₂_	_carrot, minced_
_2_	_teaspoons Italian parsley, chopped_
_¹/₄_	_cup Nayonaise®_
_4_	_garlic cloves, minced_
_¹/₄_	_teaspoon sherry vinegar_
_2_	_teaspoons lemon juice, fresh_
_1_	_teaspoon Worcestershire sauce_
_¹/₂_	_teaspoon sea salt_
_¹/₄_	_teaspoon dry mustard_
_¹/₈_	_teaspoon hot pepper sauce_
_¹/₈_	_teaspoon pepper_

1. Marinate patties overnight (or at least 2 hours) in water to cover with kombu.

2. Crumble patties and toss with ¹/₄ cup of bread crumbs, celery, scallions, carrot and parsley.

3. Blend rest of ingredients and add to tofu mix.

4. Place remaining crumbs in a shallow bowl.

5. Scoop a heaping tablespoon of mix and form patties ¹/₂-inch thick.

6. Coat with bread crumbs and lay on waxed paper on cookie sheet.

7. Refrigerate up to 2 hours.

8. Heat a skillet on medium, spray with butter or olive oil and sauté about 3 minutes each side until golden.

9. Transfer to a rack over a baking sheet and keep warm in oven until ready to serve.

10. Serve with sherry sauce and lemon wedges.

* Available by mail order from Natural Lifestyle Supplies, 800-752-2775.

SHERRY SAUCE

Makes 1 cup
5 minutes

³/₄ cup Nayonaise®
1   garlic clove, minced
1 ¹/₂ tablespoons lemon juice, fresh
1   teaspoon sherry vinegar
¹/₈ teaspoon hot pepper sauce
¹/₂ teaspoon sea salt
2   tablespoons olive oil
¹/₂ cup (amazake) milk

1. Blend all ingredients thoroughly.

> **The average hamburger made from cattle raised in the rain-forest requires the destruction of tropical forest (and the thousands of life forms it supports) equal to the size of an average kitchen.**

BURGER QUEEN WITH FRENCH FRIES

Serves 4
30 minutes

7	_tablespoons olive oil_
2	_medium onions, thinly sliced_
$^1/_2$	_teaspoon salt_
$^1/_2$	_teaspoon white pepper_
1	_teaspoon maple syrup_
1	_cup beef stock (pg 18) OR_
$^1/_4$	_cup soy sauce AND_
$^3/_4$	_cup water AND_
1	_clove garlic, finely chopped_
4	_four-oz (tempeh) burger patties_
4	_burger buns_
4	_large leaves of lettuce_
1	_tomato, thinly sliced_
4	_teaspoons Nayonaise®_

1. Heat 2 tablespoons of olive oil in a skillet. Add onions and sauté for about 2 minutes until lightly browned and transparent. Add salt and pepper and simmer, stirring occasionally, for 20 – 25 minutes until onions are golden and very soft. Stir in maple syrup.

2. Combine soy sauce, water and chopped garlic. Let sit for about 5 minutes (or use beef stock if already made up).

3. Heat remainder of olive oil in a sauté pan or skillet. Place patty in oil; brown on one side (about 5 minutes), turn and brown the other side. When the second side is nearly done, pour the soy sauce/ garlic mixture over the patties; allow to simmer until liquid has almost evaporated. Turn patties and let other side absorb remainder of the liquid. Continue cooking until outside is slightly crispy, or transfer to a grill and heat each side 4 minutes.

4. To assemble your Burger Queen: lightly spread some Nayonaise® on one half of bun. Place patty on other half. Spoon a small amount of onions on top of patty, add a slice of tomato and a lettuce leaf, top off with the other half of the bun.

Variation

Try using some sunflower greens instead of lettuce.

BAKED FRENCH FRIES

Fries are a good example of American food items being exported and returning later to our shores with a new cooking angle: the Incas never did deep fry their potatoes in oil so they never experienced the joys of the chip (from England) or the French Fry. Our version has the same edge, but is baked.

Serves 4 - 6
10 minutes plus 25 minutes baking

1	*teaspoon salt*
2	*teaspoons paprika powder*
¹/₄	*teaspoon cayenne powder*
1	*teaspoon black pepper*
4	*pounds potatoes*
	Olive oil spray

1. Preheat oven to 425° F.
2. Combine sea salt, paprika, cayenne and black pepper. Mix well.
3. Cut potatoes in ¹/₂" wedges or fingers. Rinse off excess starch with cold water and pat dry.
4. Place potato wedges on cookie tray, spray with olive oil and sprinkle lightly with spice mixture.
5. Bake 25 minutes, turning occasionally, until potatoes golden and crispy.

FISH STIX OR FINGERS

Unless we mellow out on fish consumption,
there won't be any fish left in the ocean.
(Some people may well yawn, but. . . .)

Serves 4
10 minutes plus 60 minutes marinating and baking

2   *cups (soy) milk*
2   *teaspoons sea salt*
1   *teaspoon black pepper*
2   *tablespoons olive oil*
4   *four-oz (tempeh) patties, cut into 1-inch strips*
$^1/_2$ *cup cornmeal*
$^1/_2$ *cup crushed corn flakes*
1   *teaspoon thyme*

1. Combine milk, salt, pepper and oil. Marinate patties in this mixture for about 30 minutes.

2. Preheat oven to 375° F.

3. Combine cornmeal, crushed corn flakes and thyme. Dip patties in this mixture until well coated on both sides.

4. Place patties on a lightly greased cookie sheet. Bake 15 minutes, turn and bake the other side for an additional 15 minutes until golden and crispy.

5. Serve with French fries and tartar sauce.

FISH FILLETS

These fish fillets taste great when served on buns with tartar sauce (recipe follows). Or have them with baked French fries (pg 40).

Serves 4
20 minutes plus 15 minutes steeping

6   *ounces coconut milk*
4   *cloves garlic, finely chopped*
¹/₂ cup water
1 ¹/₂ teaspoons sea salt
1 ¹/₂ teaspoons coriander
16 oz fish fillets (pg 22)
1   cup unbleached white flour
¹/₂ cup vegetable oil

   1. Combine the milk, garlic, water, salt and coriander in a bowl or blender. Whisk thoroughly. Let stand for at least 10 minutes, to meld flavors.
   2. Soak fillets in this mixture for about 5 minutes; then dust with flour until both sides are well coated.
   3. Heat oil in medium saucepan or skillet; when hot, add fillets and fry on both sides until golden brown.
   4. Remove and drain well on paper towels.

Low Fat Variation

(10 minutes plus 30 minutes baking)

   Use the same ingredients as above, but substitute 2 tablespoons of olive oil for the ¹/₂ cup vegetable oil. Preheat your oven to 375° F. Take the flour-dusted fillets and place on a lightly-oiled baking sheet. Drizzle with olive oil and bake at 375° F for 15 minutes. Turn fillets over and bake another 10 – 15 minutes or until golden brown and crispy.

TARTAR SAUCE

Makes 1 cup
5 minutes

1   *cup Nayonaise®*
¹/₄ *cup onions, finely chopped*
2   *tablespoons capers*
¹/₂ *lemon, juiced*
1   *teaspoon wholegrain mustard*
1   *teaspoon maple syrup*

1. Combine ingredients in a food processor or blender and mix until emulsified.

GUMBO

Serves 4
25 minutes

3   tablespoons olive oil
1   onion, finely chopped
1   stalk celery, finely chopped
1   cup sausage, chopped (pg 20)
½   lb okra, fresh
1   28-oz can crushed tomatoes
2   ears of corn off cobb, or one 10-oz package frozen
1   teaspoon salt
½   teaspoon pepper
    Pinch saffron
    Gumbo file powder
2   cups rice, cooked

1. Heat olive oil, add onions and celery. Sauté over medium high for 3 – 4 minutes. Add sausage, sauté 2 – 3 minutes. Add okra and stir in tomatoes and corn, salt, pepper and saffron. Simmer 10 minutes.

2. Serve over cooked rice.

Note: Some chile peppers can be added to this recipe.

NEW ENGLAND CLAM CHOWDER

Serves 4

10 minutes plus 50 minutes simmering

_3_	_tablespoons olive oil_
_1_	_medium onion, finely chopped_
_3_	_medium potatoes, peeled and cubed_
_¹/₂_	_cup water_
_2_	_four-oz fish fillets (pg 22), cut into ¹/₂-inch cubes_
_2_	_cups (soy) milk_
_¹/₄_	_teaspoon white pepper_
1 ¹/₂ teaspoons salt	

1. Heat oil in a heavy skillet, add onion and sauté 8 - 10 minutes on medium until transparent and lightly browned.

2. Add potatoes and water, cover and simmer 10 minutes.

3. Add fillets, re-cover and simmer 10 minutes.

4. Add milk, pepper and salt and simmer very lightly for 20 minutes.

"Chowder" comes from the French, "faire la chaudiere," meaning "to make a soup from oddments of fish and biscuit." The word "chaudiere" refers to the large, iron pot that returning French fishermen used to throw some of their catch into so they could all share the meal. Chowders are chunky soups; while they were originally thickened with stale bread or crackers, potatoes are used nowadays.

SPLIT PEA SOUP

Serves 4
20 minutes plus 60 minutes simmering

3	*tablespoons olive oil*
2	*onions, finely chopped*
4-5	*cloves of garlic, thinly sliced*
1	*large carrot, finely chopped*
2	*cups dried split peas, green or yellow*
6	*cups water*
2 ½	*teaspoons salt*
1	*teaspoon black pepper*
1 ½	*cups of chopped sausage (pg 20)*

1. In soup pot, heat olive oil. Add onions and garlic, sauté until transparent and lightly browned, about 2 minutes. Add carrots and sauté another minute.

2. Rinse peas and add to onion & garlic carrot mixture. Sauté another minute or two.

3. Add water, salt and pepper and slowly bring to the boil. Simmer for an hour.

4. Let cool slightly and process or blend half soup. Return to pot and mix thoroughly.

5. Stir in sausage.

Serve hot on a cold day!

MACARONI & CHEESE

Serves 4 - 6
30 minutes plus 15 minutes baking

1	*pound elbow macaroni*
2	*tablespoons olive oil*
1	*onion, finely sliced*
1/2	*teaspoon salt*
1	*cup (soy) cheddar cheese, grated*
1 1/2	*cups (soy) milk*
1/2	*cup grated, (soy) parmesan*
	Parsley to taste, finely chopped

1. Boil macaroni according to package instructions.

2. Heat olive oil in skillet or sauté pan. Sauté the onions on medium about 10 minutes, stirring occasionally. Add salt and continue sautéing until onions are well cooked and slightly crispy (about 10 more minutes).

3. Preheat oven to 350°.

4. In a small saucepan, combine cheddar, milk and most of the parmesan. Melt and mix over a low flame.

5. In an 8x13 baking dish, combine all ingredients and mix thoroughly.

6. Bake uncovered at 350° F for 15 minutes.

7. Serve sprinkled with remainder of the grated parmesan and freshly chopped parsley.

Sandwiches were invented by the staff of Lord Sandwich in southern England a couple of centuries ago. It was their solution to feeding him at the gambling table so he could gamble through lunch and dinner. Sandwiches have been a staple in lunch boxes around the world ever since.

TURKEY CLUB SANDWICH

Serves 4
15 minutes

2   *tablespoons olive oil*
4   *shallots, thinly sliced*
$^1/_2$ *pound (seitan) turkey (pp 16 & 18), very thinly sliced*
$^1/_4$ *teaspoon sea salt*
12   *slices of bread (your choice)*
4   *tablespoons Nayonaise®*
4   *large lettuce leaves*
1   *tomato, sliced thinly*
4   *slices (soy) cheese (optional)*

1. In a sauté pan, heat olive oil. Add shallots and sauté until lightly browned and transparent. Add turkey and brown on both sides, about 5 minutes. Add salt and continue to brown for another 2 minutes, turning occasionally. Remove from heat.

2. Lightly toast slices of bread.

3. Spread some Nayonaise® on the bread slices. Layer with lettuce, tomato, cheese (optional) and sauted turkey slices; top with a second slice of toast, then add more turkey, lettuce and tomato; top with third slice of bread.

4. Cut in diagonal quarters; secure with toothpicks.

CHICKEN SALAD

Serves 4
5 minutes

1   cup Nayonaise®
2   tablespoons Grey Poupon mustard
$^1/_4$ cup pickle relish
$^3/_4$ teaspoon celery seed
1   lb shredded (seitan) chicken (pp 16 & 19)
1 $^1/_2$ cups celery, chopped
$^1/_3$ cup parsley
$^1/_2$ red onion, chopped

1. Mix first four ingredients, then add the rest.

Variation

Omit the relish and instead add 1 $^1/_2$ cups of chopped Granny Smith apples and $^1/_2$ cup of chopped walnuts for a delicious Waldorf Salad.

EGG SALAD SANDWICH

Makes 4 sandwiches
10 minutes plus sitting time

1	*pound firm tofu*
2	*tablespoons Nayonaise®*
¹/₄	*onion, minced*
2	*tablespoons chopped parsley*
¹/₄	*cup celery, minced*
1 ¹/₂	*teaspoons salt*
¹/₄	*teaspoon pepper*
2	*tablespoons minced dill pickle*
1	*tablespoon mustard*
2	*tablespoons (soy) milk*
2	*tablespoons tarragon vinegar*
8	*slices bread of your choice*
4	*large lettuce leaves*
1	*tomato, sliced*

1. Combine all ingredients (except bread, lettuce, and tomato); blend until mixture reaches consistency of egg salad. Let sit several hours if possible to develop flavors.

2. Serve on bread garnished with lettuce and tomato slices.

BLT

Makes 4 sandwiches
20 minutes

1   *cup beef stock (pg 18) OR*
¹/₄   *cup soy sauce AND*
³/₄   *cup water AND*
1   *clove garlic, finely chopped*

2   *four-oz (tempeh) patties*
2   *tablespoons olive oil*
8   *slices of bread, toasted*
4   *teaspoons Nayonaise®*
1   *large avocado, sliced*
4   *large lettuce leaves*
1   *large tomato, sliced thinly*
     Alfalfa sprouts

1. If no beef stock in supply, combine soy sauce, water and chopped garlic. Let sit for about 5 minutes.

2. Slice patties in half horizontally, then cut in 2" strips.

3. In a sauté pan, heat olive oil. Add patty strips and sauté for about 4 minutes, turning regularly to ensure strips are done on both sides. Add soy mix or beef stock and simmer until all liquid has evaporated. Be sure to turn the strips from time to time to ensure liquid soaks in on both sides. Continue sauteing until the surfaces become slightly crisp; or transfer to a grill and heat each side about 4 minutes.

5. Lightly toast the bread slices.

6. Spread Nayonaise® on toast. Layer with avocado slices, patty strips, lettuce, tomato and sprouts; top with the second piece of toast. Slice diagonally and use a toothpick to hold the halves together if needed.

REUBEN SANDWICH

Serves 4
25 minutes

2   *tablespoons soy sauce**
1/3 *cup water**
1   *clove of garlic, finely chopped**
5   *tablespoons of olive oil*
4   *four-oz (tempeh) patties*
1   *medium onion, thinly sliced*
1/4 *teaspoon sea salt*
10 *oz sauerkraut, drained of excess liquid*
1   *teaspoon caraway seeds*
8   *slices rye bread*
2   *teaspoons whole grain mustard*
2   *teaspoons Nayonaise®*
1   *large tomato, thinly sliced*
4   *slices Swiss (soy) cheese (optional)*

1. If no beef stock to hand, combine soy sauce, water and chopped garlic. Mix thoroughly. Let sit for 5 minutes.

2. Heat 3 tablespoons of oil in a sauté pan on medium high and sauté patties 4 minutes each side until golden. When second side is nearly done, add soy mix or beef stock and cook until liquid has almost evaporated. Turn and allow other side to absorb remainder of liquid; continue to cook until the outside is slightly crispy.

3. In a sauté pan, heat remainder of oil. Add the onions and sauté 4 minutes, adding salt after 2 minutes. Add sauerkraut and caraway seeds. Cook for an additional 15 minutes over medium low heat.

4. Lightly toast rye bread slices. Spread whole grain mustard on one slice of bread, Nayonaise® on the other. Place sauted patty on top of one of the bread slices, add cheese (optional) and tomato slices; spoon on some of the hot sauerkraut. Top with the other slice of bread. Slice in half and use toothpicks if needed to secure the sandwich halves.

* May substitute 1/2 cup beef stock (pg 18).

HAWAIIAN CHICKEN SANDWICHES

Serves 6
20 minutes

2   *tablespoons soy sauce**
$^1/_3$ *cup water**
1   *clove of garlic, finely chopped**
3   *tablespoons olive oil*
4   *four-oz (tempeh) patties*
$^2/_3$ *cup celery*
$^1/_3$ *cup Nayonaise®*
1   *teaspoon salt*
$^1/_4$ *teaspoon white pepper*
$^1/_4$ *cup pecans or walnuts*
12 *pineapple rings, drained***
2   *tablespoons maple syrup*
12 *slices of whole grain raisin bread (or other bread)*

1. Combine soy sauce, water and chopped garlic. Let sit for about 5 minutes.

2. Heat olive oil medium high in a skillet. Fry patties until golden (5 minutes one side and 3 minutes on other). When the second side is nearly done, add soy mixture and cook until liquid has almost evaporated, then turn and allow other side to absorb the remainder of the liquid. Continue cooking until patties are slightly crispy.

3. Cube patties and combine with remaining ingredients (except bread) in a large mixing bowl. Blend thoroughly.

4. Spread this mixture on bread. Cut in half diagonally and use toothpicks to secure.

* May substitute with $^1/_2$ cup of beef stock (pg 18).
** Use fresh pineapple if available.

MEXICAN COOK COLLECTING TOMATOES FOR HIS "SALSA VERDE":

FRAPAR

CHAPTER FIVE

South of the Border

There's a whole range of cuisines south of the border. Their beauty lies in the simple ingredients and preparations.

First of all, let's look at some salsas for use with almost any dish.

SALSA FRESCA

Makes 4 cups
15 minutes

4	medium tomatoes, finely chopped
1	medium onion, finely chopped
1	bunch cilantro, chopped
$^1/_2$	teaspoon dried, crushed, red chile peppers
1	fresh Anaheim chile, finely chopped
1	teaspoon sea salt
$^1/_2$	tablespoon black pepper
1	lime, juiced

1. Mix ingredients in bowl. Let sit a few minutes to allow juices and flavors to combine.

Salsa fresca is best used the same day, but it can be kept covered in the fridge overnight.

The Anaheim chile is bright green, although it turns red as it ripens. It is about 6 inches long, with a pointed end. It has a mild to medium-hot flavor. Dried, they are often labeled California or New Mexico chiles.

Cilantro is also sometimes called Chinese parsley or coriander. It has a strong flavor and characteristic smell which some may not appreciate (in which case, regular parsley could be substituted).

SALSA FRESCA CON CORN

Makes 5 cups

Add the kernels of two ears of fresh corn to the basic Salsa Fresca recipe (p. 55). Frozen corn can be substituted if fresh is not available or if you are in a hurry.

GUACAMOLE

The Aztecs combined mashed avocado with chili peppers to make "Guacamole," meaning "avocado mixture." The Spanish added citrus and cilantro to create the complex dip or sauce that we know today.

Makes 1 ¹/₂ cups
10 minutes

2   *large, ripe avocados*
1   *cup cilantro, chopped*
1   *lime, juiced*
1   *teaspoon sea salt*
1   *small tomato, chopped*
10 *drops of picante (hot) sauce*

1. Peel avocados; remove seeds and set one aside.
2. Mash avocados with fork until slightly chunky.
3. Mix in other ingredients.
4. Place reserved seed on top (to prevent mix from turning brown), cover and refrigerate.

TVP is widely used south of the border as a meat substitute.

CHICKEN & SPINACH ENCHILADA

Serves 6 (2 enchiladas per person)
30 minutes and 25 minutes baking

1   *cup (TVP) chicken chunks*
1   *cup chicken stock (pg 19)*
2   *10-oz packages of spinach OR 2 bunches of fresh spinach*
2   *bunches green onions*
1   *tablespoon olive oil*
$^1/_4$ *teaspoon sea salt*
1   *dozen corn tortillas*
$^1/_3$ *cup corn oil (as needed)*
1   *cup grated soy Jack cheese (optional)*
2   *cups salsa verde (follows)*

1. Combine chicken chunks and stock in a pan, bring to a boil and let sit 10 minutes. When cooled, pull each apart by hand, creating a texture resembling shredded chicken.

2. Wash spinach and place wet leaves in large pot; cover and steam on medium heat until spinach wilts, about 3 – 4 minutes. Remove and put in strainer to drain excess water. Let cool, then chop.

3. Clean and trim ends of green onions; cut into thirds. Toss with olive oil and sea salt; grill or broil until lightly browned.

4. Heat enough oil to cover bottom of small sauté pan; fry tortillas for about 20 seconds on each side until pliable and easy to handle without breaking or tearing.

5. Pre-heat oven to 375° F.

6. Fill each tortilla with two tablespoons of chopped spinach and 3 or 4 pieces of green onion; sprinkle some grated Jack cheese on top if desired. Roll tortillas up into cigar shapes.

7. Place enchiladas in a lightly greased 13x8 inch baking pan.

8. Repeat steps 5 and 6 for remaining tortillas and pour salsa verde over the top.

9. Cover pan with baking foil and bake for 20 to 25 minutes.

SALSA VERDE

Tomatillos are small green tomatoes wrapped in papery husks. They can be found fresh in the produce section of a supermarket, or canned in the Mexican food section.

Makes 3 cups
25 minutes

1   *pound tomatillos*
¹/₂ pound tomatoes, peeled
3   *garlic cloves, peeled and chopped*
1   *bunch cilantro, chopped*
1   *teaspoon sea salt*

1. Preheat oven to 450° F.
2. Dehusk tomatillos and put on a baking tray. Roast until blistered and well browned. If you listen carefully, the tomatillos will pop and "sing" when they are done!
3. Put grilled tomatillos in blender with peeled tomatoes, garlic, cilantro and sea salt; puree. Spoon this mixture into a bowl and cover.

Salsa Verde can be kept in the fridge for a few days if needed.

The Mexican tortilla is made from dried corn (hominy) that has been soaked in lime and then ground into a dough called "masa." It is then pressed flat and baked. The New World tradition of unleavened breads was only changed when Europeans brought gluten-rich wheat and yeast to create raised, light breads. Served soft, tortillas are wrapped around various fillings to create quesadillas, burritos, and enchiladas. Fried crisp, they are used as taco shells, tostadas, and chips to go with salsa.

ENCHILADAS COLORADO

An enchilada is a soft, corn tortilla wrapped around a filling and baked in a sauce. Usually the filling is plain (cheese, chicken, or beef) and bland, while the sauce is traditionally the spicier element.

Serves 6 (2 enchiladas each)
30 minutes plus 30 minutes baking

3	*tablespoons olive oil*
1	*medium onion, chopped fine*
1	*medium carrot, sliced*
1	*red bell pepper, finely chopped*
1	*zucchini, sliced in half lengthwise then cut into half-moons, 1/4-inch thick*
1	*stalk of broccoli, cut into small florets*
2	*ears of fresh corn, kernels off cobb (or 10 oz frozen corn)*
1	*teaspoon sea salt*
1/2	*teaspoon black pepper*
1 1/2	*cups (seitan) pork (pg 19) (optional)*
1	*dozen corn tortillas*
1/2	*cup corn oil*
2	*cups of Colorado Sauce (pg 61)*

1. Heat olive oil in large sauté pan. Add onion and sauté until lightly browned and transparent, about 3 minutes.

2. Add carrot and bell pepper and sauté another 2-3 minutes, stirring occasionally.

3. Add remaining vegetables, salt, pepper, and pork if used. Sauté 4 to 5 minutes over medium heat, stirring constantly to prevent sticking or burning. Cover and set aside until tortillas are ready.

4. In small sauté pan, heat 1 tablespoon corn oil (enough to cover bottom of pan). Fry tortillas for 3 – 5 seconds on each side until soft. Add more corn oil as needed for the remainder of the tortillas, but no more than 1 tablespoon at a time. Stack tortillas and set aside.

5. Pre-heat oven to 375° F.

6. Put 1 1/2 cups Colorado sauce in a shallow bowl or pie pan. Line up tortillas, Colorado sauce, a working plate, vegetable filling and a lightly greased 13x8 inch baking pan.

7. Dip each tortilla in Colorado sauce until well coated on both sides. Lay on work plate. Spoon filling in center of tortilla. Spoon a little extra Colorado sauce on top and roll tortilla into cigar shape. Place tortillas seam down in the baking pan.

8. Repeat steps 7 and 8 for remaining tortillas.

9. Spread remaining Colorado sauce from bowl on top of enchiladas.

10. Cover pan with baking foil and bake for 25 to 30 minutes.

11. Serve with $1/2$ cup of Colorado sauce for condiment.

Variations

Add a sprinkling of grated Jack or Cheddar soy cheese on top of the filling before rolling the tortilla, and/or on top of the finished enchiladas just before baking.

Serve with a dollop of Fresh Corn Salsa (pg 56) and use blue corn tortillas if you can find them.

COLORADO SAUCE (spicy)

Standing in front of a bank of ten or more different types of unlabelled chile peppers in the supermarket can result in a mild state of panic and a frantic search for the Produce Manager to identify the one chile in that day's recipe.

The Pasilla chile is mild to medium hot, chocolate brown, thin and about 6 inches long. It is usually bought dried, at which time it is black in color and sometimes labeled Chile Negro. It is occasionally mislabelled "poblano" or "ancho," but these are different chiles, so don't be thrown by them.

Makes 3 cups
10 minutes, plus 30 minutes baking

1   package (2 oz) dried, mild Pasilla chilies
2   pounds tomatillos
5   garlic cloves, chopped
$^{1}/_{2}$ cup filtered water
1   teaspoon sea salt

1. Pre-heat oven to 450° F. Place chilies on baking tray or cookie sheet and roast until browned and puffed, about 2 minutes each side. When cooled, deseed and remove stems.

2. Dehusk tomatillos and roast for about 10 to 15 minutes in same oven until blistered on both sides.

3. Place chile pods, tomatillos and garlic in blender and puree. Add a little more water if mixture becomes too thick.

4. Add sea salt to taste and pour mixture into shallow bowl. Cover.

99 CENTS BURRITO

Serves 6 (1 Burrito each)
40 minutes

1	*cup (TVP) beef chunks*
1	*cup beef stock (pg 18)*
1	*medium potato, boiled and cut into ¹/₂-inch squares*
3 - 4	*tablespoons of olive oil*
1	*Spanish onion, chopped*
1	*red bell pepper, finely chopped*
1	*Anaheim chile, finely chopped*
2	*teaspoons of cumin*
1	*teaspoon chile powder*
1	*bunch green onions, thinly sliced*
1	*cup Colorado sauce (pg 61)*
1	*teaspoon sea salt*
6	*burrito-size whole-wheat tortillas*
1	*cup Salsa Fresca (pg 55)*

1. Combine beef chunks and stock in a pot, bring to boil and let sit 10 minutes. When cooled, pull each apart by hand, creating a texture resembling shredded beef.

2. Boil potato in water till fork tender.

3. Heat olive oil in large sauté pan over medium high heat. When hot, add onion and sauté until transparent, about 3 minutes. Add bell peppers and chiles, sauté for 2 minutes; add beef, cumin and chile powder, sauté 5 minutes. Add potatoes, green onions, Colorado sauce and salt; lower heat and simmer for another 3 to 4 minutes to allow flavors to blend, stirring occasionally.

4. In ungreased skillet, heat tortillas about 20 seconds on one side; turn over and heat for another 5 seconds until softened.

5. On flat surface, lay out heated tortillas. Spoon some filling in center of lower half of each tortilla, top with some Salsa Fresca. Fold right side of tortilla over; roll tortilla up from bottom towards top, creating a cigar shape that can be held by hand easily.

Variations

Add a sprinkling of Cheddar or Jack soy cheese, guacamole and/or hot sauce.

TAMALES

Tamales are made by spreading a thin layer of masa on a dried corn husk; adding a meat or cheese filling; then tying the husk into a neat bundle for steam-cooking. Favorite Southwestern tamales include small "tamalitos," often served alongside barbecued "meats" and "green" tamales made with fresh summer corn. Our tamales are the smaller Guatemalan versions. Corn masa is usually available fresh at your local Mexican or Southwestern specialty stores.

Serves 10 (4 small tamales per person)
45 minutes and 45 minutes cooking

1	*package dried, corn husks*
$^{1}/_{2}$	*pound tomatoes*
3	*cups Colorado Sauce (pg 61)*
2	*pounds corn masa*
$^{3}/_{4}$	*cup corn oil*

1. Soak corn husks in warm water until slightly softened (about 15 minutes).

2. Peel and puree tomatoes. Blend thoroughly with Colorado Sauce. Pour sauce mixture into masa, blending by hand. Gradually add corn oil until mixture has a consistency of smooth dough.

3. Take a corn husk and lay flat on a smooth surface. Starting about 2 inches from the narrower bottom of husk, spread maximum $^{1}/_{4}$-inch thick by about 3 inch wide layer of masa mix along center of husk, ending one inch from the wider top.

4. Add your choice of filling (follows) on top of the masa mix. Fold in bottom part of husk one-third of the way, and roll remainder of husk from left to right into a thick, cigar-shaped roll. Repeat for remainder of husks.

5. Place stainless steel colander (or steamer) in bottom of a 5 quart pot and fill with water to just below base of colander. Place tamales next to each other, standing upright on colander.

6. Bring water to boil, cover and steam for 45 minutes, occasionally adding water as needed.

BEEF AND CHILE FILLING

2   *cups (TVP) beef chunks*
1 ³/₄ *cups beef stock (pg 18)*
1   *can (7 ounces) chopped green chiles*
1   *cup shredded Jack or cheddar cheese (optional)*

1. Combine beef and stock in a pot, bring to boil and let sit 10 minutes.

2. When cooled, shred the TVP chunks by hand into a texture resembling shredded beef. Mix with the green chiles.

3. Add 1 tablespoon of above mix and 1 teaspoon of cheese.

SWEET POTATO AND CORN FILLING

10 minutes plus 40 minutes baking

3   large sweet potatoes
4   ears of fresh corn (or 1 pound of frozen corn, thawed)

1. Preheat oven to 375° F.

2. Wash and clean sweet potatoes. Bake at 375° F for about 40 minutes. Cool, peel and mash.

3. If using fresh corn, dehusk and boil for 5 minutes. Let cool and cut kernels off the cobb into a bowl.

4. Mix corn and mashed sweet potatoes together, cover and set aside.

TACOS

In this recipe we use soft shelled tortillas. However, you can use pre-made, hard shelled tacos for a crunchy texture.

Serves 6 (2 tacos per person)
20 minutes

1   *dozen corn tortillas*
1 ¹/₂ *cups Salsa Fresca (pg 55)*
2   *cups white cabbage, finely sliced*

1. On dry griddle or sauté pan, heat tortillas for about 20 seconds on each side; tortillas should be soft and pliable.
2. Place tortillas on flat work surface; fill each taco with one of the fillings below.
3. Add some Salsa Fresca and sliced white cabbage. Fold tortillas in half.

Variations

Add sprinkling of Jack or cheddar soy cheese on top of hot filling (in addition to Salsa Fresca and cabbage).

Use Guacamole (see pg 56) instead of or in addition to Salsa Fresca.

Beef Taco Filling

1   *cup (TVP) ground beef*
1   *cup beef stock (pg 18)*
2   *tablespoons of olive oil*
1   *onion, finely chopped*
3   *garlic cloves, finely chopped*
2   *teaspoons cumin*
1   *teaspoon chile powder*
     sea salt

65

1. Combine beef and stock in a pot, bring to boil and let sit 10 minutes.

2. In sauté pan or skillet, heat olive oil; sauté garlic with chopped onion until transparent (about 3 minutes). Add beef, spices and salt to taste. Lower heat and simmer for another 3 to 4 minutes to allow flavors to be absorbed. Cover and set aside.

Taco Filling (Simplistico)

4   four-oz (tempeh) patties

1. Follow basic tempeh pattie preparation steps (pg 39).
2. Cut each tempeh pattie into 6 strips and place two strips in each taco.

Taco Filling (Picante)

4   four-oz (tempeh) patties
2   teaspoons cumin
¹/₂   teaspoon sea salt
¹/₂   teaspoon crushed red chiles

1. Follow basic tempeh preparation steps (pg 39).
2. Crumble tempeh and put in mixing bowl. Add spices and work into tempeh with fingers until mixture reaches coarse ground-meat consistency.

TACO SALAD

Serves 2
25 minutes

½   *cup (TVP) minced beef*
½   *cup beef stock (pg 18)*
2   *corn tortillas, sliced into thin strips*
2   *tablespoons olive oil*
½   *onion, chopped*
2   *cloves garlic, finely chopped*
1   *teaspoon cumin*
½   *teaspoon chile powder*
    Sea salt
½   *head of butter lettuce, shredded*
1   *cup white cabbage, shredded*
1   *cup cilantro, chopped*
4   *radishes, thinly sliced*
1   *tomato, chopped*
1   *ear fresh corn (or 1 cup of frozen corn, thawed)*
1   *cup sliced cucumber*
½   *Cilantro Vinaigrette (follows)*
½   *ripe avocado, cut into slices just before serving*

1. Combine beef and stock in a pot, bring to a boil and let sit 10 minutes.

2. Preheat oven to 350° F. Place tortilla strips in oven and bake for 10 to 15 minutes until crispy. Take out and let cool. Cover and set aside.

3. In sauté pan, heat oil and sauté onions and garlic until lightly browned. Add beef, spices and sea salt to taste. Simmer on low heat for 5 minutes until the flavors are absorbed. Remove from heat and set aside to cool.

4. Combine remaining (salad) ingredients in large bowl and toss well. Top with warm beef mixture. Sprinkle crisp corn (tortilla) chips over salad and drizzle with cilantro vinaigrette.

5. Garnish with avocado slices just before serving.

Cilantro and Lime Vinaigrette

Makes 2 $^1/_2$ cups
5 minutes and 10 minutes sitting

$^1/_4$ *red onion, coarsely chopped*
$^1/_2$ *cup lime juice (about 4 limes)*
$^1/_4$ *cup white wine vinegar*
1 $^1/_2$ *cups olive oil*
2   *tablespoons cumin*
2   *teaspoons sea salt*
1   *cup chopped cilantro*

1. Puree red onion, lime juice and vinegar in blender. Add olive oil, cumin, and salt, blending until emulsified. Add cilantro and mix in.
2. Let sit for a few minutes to develop flavors.

MEXICAN LASAGNA

This recipe was made for an Italian guest who wanted "something Mexican." He was not disappointed.

Serves 8
40 minutes and 1 hour baking

3   *tablespoons Canola oil*
2   *medium Spanish onions, finely chopped*
6   *large garlic cloves, finely chopped*
2   *tablespoons ground cumin*
1   *handful fresh oregano*
4   *cups (seitan) beef (or reconstituted TVP chunks),*
    shredded (pp 16 & 18)
12 *corn tortillas*
10 *cups Chile sauce (follows)*
1   *lb shredded soy cheese (or ¹/₂ lb dairy cheese)*

1. In a sauté pan, heat canola oil; sauté onion and garlic for a couple of minutes until lightly brown. Add cumin, oregano, seitan and sauté a few more minutes. Cool and set aside. If using TVP chunks, reconstitute and shred by hand to resemble shredded beef.

2. Make the sauce (below).

3. Dry-fry tortillas on hot skillet for about 30 seconds on each side. Cut into lasagna-width strips. Set aside.

4. Preheat oven to 350° F.

5. In 12x9 baking dish, layer ingredients in this order: a) chile sauce, b) tortillas, c) seitan mix, d) cheese. Repeat sequence and top with an ample layer of sauce. Reserve some of sauce as condiment when serving dish.

6. Bake Lasagna for 45 minutes; let stand a further 15 minutes before serving.

Chile Sauce

1   *cup unbleached flour*
4   *teaspoons garlic powder*
1   *teaspoon sea salt*
1   *teaspoon fresh ground pepper*
1   *cup canola oil*
4   *large Spanish onions, chopped fine*
12 *mild chiles, deseeded, chopped fine*
12 *hot chiles, deseeded, chopped fine*
8   *cups of vegetable stock*

1. In a large bowl, mix flour, garlic and seasoning; gradually stir in enough canola oil to make a thick paste.

2. Heat 3 tablespoons of canola oil in a large frying pan; sauté the chopped onions until transparent. Add chiles and sauté for another three minutes.

3. Slowly stir flour paste into vegetable mix and cook for a few minutes. Gradually add vegetable stock, stirring constantly. Bring to boil, lower heat and simmer for approximately ten minutes, stirring occasionally. Add more stock if sauce becomes too thick.

FAJITAS

Serves 4 - 6
30 minutes

1	_pound (seitan) beef (pp 16 & 18), thinly sliced_
3	_limes, juiced_
2	_teaspoons sea salt_
4	_tablespoons olive oil_
1	_red onion, sliced thinly_
1	_red bell pepper, sliced thinly_
1	_yellow bell pepper, sliced thinly_
2	_teaspoons cumin seed_
1	_teaspoon ground coriander powder_
1	_tomato, chopped_
1	_dozen corn tortillas_

1. Marinate sliced beef in a mixture of lime juice and 1 teaspoon of sea salt. (15 minutes)

2. In large cast-iron skillet or sauté pan, heat olive oil; add sliced onion and sauté for 2 minutes. Add bell peppers, spices and 1 teaspoon sea salt and sauté 3 – 4 minutes. Add seitan and sauté 3 – 4 minutes. Add and sauté tomatoes another 3 – 4 minutes, stirring constantly.

3. Dry-fry the tortillas in a heated skillet on medium high, 20 seconds one side and 5 seconds the flip side.

4. Heap the filling on top of tortilla; or eat filling and tortilla separately; or use the tortilla as a spoon. Serve with Salsa Fresca (pg 55) and Guacamole (pg 56).

REFRIED BEANS

For this old standby, we used black beans, but any will do.

Serves 6 - 8
20 minutes and 3 hours cooking

2   *cups black beans*
8   *cups of water*
1   *medium onion, cut in quarters*
3   *bay leaves*
5   *garlic cloves, peeled*
1 ½ *teaspoons sea salt*
4   *tablespoons olive oil*
4   *garlic cloves, chopped finely*
1   *teaspoon cumin (optional)*
     Sea salt

1. Pick beans clean of debris and rinse until the water runs clear. Soak overnight in 8 cups of water (or bring beans and water to a boil for 2 minutes and set off heat for 1 ½ hours).

2. In large pot add beans (including their soak water), onion, bay leaves and garlic. Bring to the boil and simmer for 1 ½ hours until tender. Then add sea salt and remove bay leaves.

3. In large sauté pan or skillet, heat olive oil, stir in cumin and then sauté chopped garlic until lightly brown.

4. Gradually add black beans and water to garlic and mash until all liquid absorbed. Add sea salt to taste. If mixture becomes too dry, add a little water or vegetable broth.

About beans: Presoaking is a device to reduce cooking time. It does not have to be done, and where the soaking water is thrown away, it wastes nutrients.

It is important when cooking beans to add salt only after the beans have been fully cooked, otherwise the beans become tough to eat.

If gas is a problem with beans, bear with it and after a few months, your system will be able to manage without gas. Or if that idea is offensive, the following works: soak beans overnight and discard the soaking liquid. Then bring fresh water to the boil and simmer for 1/2 hour; and discard this liquid, too. Add fresh water and once again bring to the boil and cook until the beans are soft.

The digestive enzyme purchasable in small bottles that claims to eliminate gas, appears to merely delay the outbreaks. But this might just get you through the dinner engagement and back home in time! Using kombu (kelp) flavors the beans and helps in their digestion.

BLACK BEAN SOUP

Serves 6
20 minutes plus 30 minutes cooking

3	tablespoons olive oil
1	medium onion, chopped
5	garlic cloves, chopped
1	teaspoon ground cumin
3	cups black beans, cooked (pg 72, steps 1 & 2)
2	cups water
1/2	teaspoon chile powder
1/2	can (6 oz) tomatillo salsa
1	bay leaf
1	cup cilantro, chopped
6	cilantro sprigs

1. Heat olive oil in large pot. Add onion, garlic, and cumin and sauté for 2 to 3 minutes, until lightly browned and transparent.

2. Add cooked black beans, then two cups of water.

3. Add chile powder, tomatillo salsa, bay leaf and chopped cilantro. Simmer for 30 minutes, stirring occasionally.

4. Put mixture in food processor or mixer; blend thoroughly.

5. Poor back into pot, reheat to just below a simmer.

6. Garnish with cilantro sprig and serve hot with corn bread still warm from the oven.

CORN BREAD

Native Americans have prepared corn purely for 6,000 years, without the eggs, fat and milk used by Europeans. We have tried to balance the simple flavor of the ancient recipe with the richness of the modern. Try using stone ground cornmeal which tastes more like corn than normally ground cornmeal.

Serves 6 to 8
15 minutes and 20 minutes baking

1	cup blue or yellow cornmeal
¹/₂	cup unbleached flour
1 ¹/₂	teaspoons baking powder
¹/₂	teaspoon sea salt
10	ounces soft or medium firm tofu, drained
¹/₂	cup water
¹/₄	cup maple syrup
1	orange, juiced
1	cup fresh (or 10 oz frozen and thawed) corn kernels
1	Anaheim chile, deseeded and finely chopped

1. Preheat oven to 425° F.

2. In a large bowl, mix cornmeal, flour, baking powder and sea salt.

3. Put tofu, water, maple syrup and orange juice in blender and puree.

4. Blend puree into flour mixture.

5. Add corn kernels and chopped chile pepper.

6. Pour dough mixture into lightly oiled cast iron skillet (8-inches diameter) and bake 20 minutes until top cracks and is golden brown.

MENUDO
A hearty soup

Serves 6 to 8
20 minutes with 30 minutes simmering

4   *tablespoons olive oil*
2   *medium onions, chopped*
8   *garlic cloves, finely chopped*
4   *teaspoons cumin*
2   *teaspoons coriander*
2   *teaspoons chile powder*
2   *cups tomato, chopped*
2   *cups thinly sliced (seitan) beef strips (pp 16 & 18)*
1   *can (29 oz) hominy*
6   *cups vegetable broth*
    Sea salt
1   *bunch cilantro, chopped*

1. Heat olive oil in large soup pot; add garlic and onions, sauté until lightly brown. Add spices, stirring for one minute.

2. Add tomatoes, beef strips and hominy. Sauté for another 3 – 4 minutes until flavors are absorbed.

3. Add vegetable broth and sea salt to taste; let simmer on low for about 30 minutes.

4. Add cilantro and adjust seasoning if needed.

5. Serve with hot corn bread.

STEAK VERA CRUZ

The Portobello mushroom is as large as a New York steak and perhaps tastier.

Serves 4 - 6
30 minutes

1 ¹/₂ cups long grain brown rice
3 ³/₄ cups water
¹/₂   teaspoon sea salt
2   bay leaves
2   large Portobello mushrooms
2   tablespoons olive oil
2   garlic cloves, minced
¹/₂   teaspoon sea salt
1   cup Vera Cruz sauce (p. 81)
1   cup cilantro, chopped

1. Rinse rice until water runs clear. In large pot, add water, sea salt, and bay leaves. Bring to boil, cover and simmer about 25 minutes.

2. Preheat grill to medium heat.

3. Separate mushroom stems from tops and slice stems in half lengthwise.

4. In a small bowl, mix minced garlic with olive oil and sea salt. Brush this mixture on both sides of mushroom tops and stems.

5. Grill mushrooms 3 minutes per side, depending on thickness of mushrooms. They should be lightly charred but still juicy. Remove from and let cool slightly. Cut mushroom tops diagonally into slices.

6. Spoon some rice in the center of a plate. Fan 3 or 4 slices of mushroom on top of the rice. Spoon 3 to 4 tablespoons of Vera Cruz sauce on top as well; garnish with cilantro leaves.

SIX LAYER TOSTADA

Serves 4 - 6
30 minutes plus 70 minutes simmering

1   *cup pinto beans*
5   *cups water*
1   *medium-sized onion, cut into quarters*
4   *bay leaves*
2   *teaspoons sea salt*
6   *corn tortillas*
1 ½ *cups Salsa Fresca (pg 55)*
1   *cup Jack cheese, grated (optional)*
2   *cups chopped tomatoes*
2   *cups white cabbage or lettuce, thinly sliced*
1   *avocado, sliced*

1. Rinse and soak Pinto beans overnight in water.

2. Add onion quarters and bay leaves. Bring to boil, lower the heat and let simmer for one hour, half covered. After an hour, test beans for doneness. They should be soft, but still slightly firm to the touch. Add salt. Simmer for another 10 minutes, so beans can absorb salt slowly. Let cool, cover and set aside.

3. Preheat oven to 375° F. Lay corn tortillas flat on a baking sheet and bake for ten minutes on each side until crisp.

4. Put tortilla on a plate and build the Tostada in layers as follows:

a) Pinto beans, b) Salsa Fresca, c) Jack cheese, d) tomato, e) cabbage or lettuce, f) avocado slice.

5. For those who like it hot, add a few drops of your favorite hot sauce.

TAQUITO

Even though you may think there's cheese in these taquitos, there isn't: the creamy texture comes from the potato.

Serves 4 (2 per person)
20 minutes plus 40 minutes boiling/baking

1	*large potato*
$1/4$	*cup coconut milk*
$1/3$	*cup roasted garlic butter (pg 23)*
1	*teaspoon sea salt*
$1/2$	*teaspoon black pepper*
$1/2$	*flour, unbleached*
$1/2$	*cup water*
$1/2$	*cup corn or olive oil*
8	*corn tortillas*

1. Peel and boil potato.
2. Mash potato with coconut milk, garlic puree and seasoning.
3. Mix flour and water into a thick paste.
4. Heat one tablespoon of oil in large skillet. Fry a tortilla for about 20 seconds on each side until softened. Remove from skillet.
5. Pre-heat oven to 375° F.
6. Place 3 to 4 tablespoons of filling on bottom half of tortilla; roll into cigar shape. Just before you get to top, spread some flour/water paste on top of tortilla—the paste will act as a glue and help seal the tortilla. Finish rolling all the way to the top.
7. Repeat procedure for rest of tortillas.
8. Place rolled-up Taquitos on lightly oiled cookie sheet.
9. Bake 20 – 25 minutes until firm and crispy.
10. Serve with Guacamole (pg 56) and/or Colorado Sauce (pg 61) as a dip.

SOUTHWEST PIZZA

Serves 1 - 2
15 minutes plus 10 minutes baking

2   *four-oz (tempeh) patties*
3   *teaspoons cumin*
$^1/_2$ *teaspoon crushed red chiles*
$^1/_2$ *teaspoon sea salt*
1   *cup Salsa Fresca (pg 55)*
$^1/_2$ *grated soy cheese of your choice (optional)*
1   *bunch cilantro, chopped*
1   *pizza crust, 10-inch diameter (pg 89)*

1. Prepare pattie according to basic recipe (pg 39).
2. Preheat oven (and pizza stone if available) to 400° F.
3. In a large bowl, crumble the pattie. Add cumin, chile peppers and salt. Blend by hand until spices are well worked in and mixture has a coarse consistency.
4. Spread Salsa Fresca on pizza crust and top with pattie mixture; sprinkle with cheese (optional).
5. Bake pizza 10 minutes or until the cheese has melted.
6. Just before serving, add chopped cilantro.

Variation

Add a dollop of fresh guacamole (pg 56) in addition to cilantro just before serving.

PASTA VERA CRUZ

Serves 4 - 5
15 minutes

1   *pound of bowtie pasta**
4 - 5 *Cups of Vera Cruz sauce (follows)*
4   *ounces of rennetless Feta Cheese***

1. Cook pasta per package instructions. Drain and put in serving bowl. Toss Vera Cruz sauce through pasta. Top with crumbled Feta cheese.

*Substitute with pasta of your choice.

**We recommend a quality organic brand of feta cheese that is hormone free and available from some health food store; or mail order from Redwood Hill Farms (1-707-823-6246) or Walnut Acres Organic Farms (1-800-433-3998).

Vera Cruz Sauce

Makes 5 cups
20 minutes

4   *tablespoons olive oil*
1   *medium onion, finely chopped*
1   *medium red bell pepper, finely chopped*
1   *green Anaheim chile, finely chopped*
1   *teaspoon cumin*
1 ½ *teaspoons sea salt*
½   *teaspoon black pepper*
2   *tomatoes, chopped*
½   *medium (or 1 small) jicama, chopped*
1   *cup chopped cilantro*

1. Heat olive oil in a sauté pan until hot. Add onions and sauté until lightly browned. Add bell peppers, chile, cumin, salt and pepper and sauté until softened, about 2 to 3 minutes. Add tomatoes and jicama. Let simmer 5 to 10 minutes on medium low heat, stirring occasionally. Let cool.

2. Garnish with cilantro just before serving.

This sauce keeps well for several days when refrigerated.

CHILE RELLENO

The Anaheim chile pepper has a delicate outer skin, (compared to, for example, a bell pepper). Therefore, when you peel the pepper, as per the instructions in this recipe, take care not to rip up the flesh of the pepper while trying to remove the skin. Don't hesitate to leave some skin attached, as not all of the skin will come off easily.

Serves 4 to 6
45 minutes

8-10 fresh Anaheim chiles
1   pound firm tofu
5   garlic cloves, minced
2   teaspoons sea salt
1   cup parsley, finely chopped
1   bunch green onions, minced
1   cup grated (soy) Jack or Mozzarella cheese (optional)
$^1/_2$ cup flour
$^1/_2$ teaspoon baking soda
1   bottle (10 oz) soda water
$^1/_2$ teaspoon sea salt
1 $^1/_2$ cups refried black beans (pg 72)
1   cup corn oil

1. Preheat broiler and roast chiles until blistered (about 5 minutes each side).

2. Drain tofu and let sit for 5 to 10 minutes in bowl. Drain again to remove excess water. Add minced garlic, sea salt, parsley, green onions (and cheese). Blend with a mixer until creamy.*

3. Mix baking soda with flour and whisk in soda water and sea salt until batter reaches a thick, yoghurt-like consistency.

4. Place roasted chiles in a brown paper bag or bowl covered with plastic until cool. Carefully peel off outer layer of charred skin and slice chile along the length of one side to remove seeds. In doing so, keep stems and pods intact if possible.

5. Spoon some of the tofu filling and refried black beans into each chile pod.

6. Heat about $^1/_2$ inch of oil in large frying pan.

7. Dip each chile in batter until well coated.

8. Carefully place in hot oil and fry for 2 to 3 minutes on each side until golden brown.

9. Serve hot, topped with Vera Cruz sauce (pg 81).

* This mixture resembles a French, herbed cream cheese in flavor and consistency. It can be made a day or two in advance, keeps well in the fridge and marinates wonderfully.

The Incas, Aztecs and Mayans realized hot peppers preserved meat, so they created the dish we know as "chile con carne" (peppers with meat).

CHAPTER SIX

Those Familiar Italian Flavors

Italian dishes are so acceptable to our palates that they have almost become a secondary American cuisine. If there is one recipe that defines Italian cooking, it is tomato sauce made the proper way.

BASIC TOMATO SAUCE

This sauce improve with age, so feel free to double the recipe and keep unused portions in the fridge for several weeks.

Makes 6-8 cups
15 minutes and 30 minutes to 2 hours simmering

$1/4$	cup olive oil
1	onion, finely chopped
8	garlic cloves, finely chopped
2	fresh, ripe tomatoes, chopped
1	28-oz can chopped tomatoes
1	tablespoon fresh thyme
1	tablespoon fresh basil
1	tablespoon fresh oregano
$1/2$	teaspoon red pepper flakes
$1/4$	cup red wine
1	tablespoon salt
1	teaspoon pepper
$1/2$	cup sake or red wine
1	cup beef stock (pg 18)

1. In a large skillet, sauté onion and garlic until transparent and lightly browned. Add fresh tomatoes and sauté 2 minutes.

2. Add remaining ingredients and simmer $1/2$ – 2 hours.

> **"Pasta" comes from the Italian word for "paste"—there are over 500 types of pasta, a tribute to the inventive Italian cuisine. Dried DeCecco is a reliable and generally available brand.**

SPAGHETTI WITH MEAT SAUCE

Serves 4 - 6
20 minutes

2	cups ground (TVP) beef
1 ³/₄	cups beef stock (pg 18)
2	tablespoons olive oil
1	medium onion, coarsely chopped
4	garlic cloves, sliced finely
¹/₂	teaspoon black pepper
4	cups basic tomato sauce (above)
1	pound spaghetti
	Grated (soy) parmesan cheese (optional)

1. Cook spaghetti per package instructions.

2. In large sauté pan, heat oil, add onions and garlic and sauté until transparent and lightly browned, about 3 minutes.

3. Add salt, pepper and dry beef, stir in well, then add stock and simmer 4 minutes. Add tomato sauce, stir well and bring to simmer.

4. Serve spaghetti topped with warm meat sauce; sprinkle with parmesan cheese if desired.

LASAGNA AL FELLINI

Serves 8
1 hour plus 1 hour baking

1	*pound lasagna noodles*
1	*pound firm tofu*
8	*garlic cloves, minced*
1	*teaspoon sea salt*
1	*cup parsley*
1	*bunch green onions*
1/2	*cup grated (soy) mozzarella or cheddar cheese (optional)*
1/2	*cup cashew pesto (pg 96)*
1 1/2	*cups minced beef (pp 16 & 18)*
4	*bunches spinach*
2	*tablespoons olive oil*
1	*medium onion, finely chopped*
4	*cups tomato sauce (pg 85)*
1/2	*cup garlic butter (pg 23)*
2	*oz grated (soy) parmesan*

1. Cook pasta according to package instructions. Drain and set aside.

2. Drain tofu and let sit 10 minutes in bowl, then drain again. In food processor, combine and blend four cloves of garlic, sea salt, parsley, green onions (and cheese). Add tofu and cashew pesto, blend until creamy and set aside.*

3. Steam and chop spinach. Set aside.

4. Heat olive oil and sauté onion with remaining garlic until transparent and lightly browned. Add ground beef, simmer 3 – 4 minutes until flavors absorbed. Add this mixture to tomato sauce and simmer 10 minutes.

5. Preheat oven to 350° F.

6. Brush 13x10 inch baking pan with garlic oil. Use the ingredients to build layers as follows: start with pasta, which is brushed with garlic oil, follow with ricotta mixture and parmesan, then tomato sauce, then spinach. Repeat these four layers until ingredients are used up. Finish with an ample layer of tomato sauce.

7. Bake covered for 45 minutes; uncover and bake for additional 15 minutes.

*This mixture resembles a French, herbed cream cheese in flavor and consistency. It can be made a day or two in advance. It keeps well in the fridge, and marinates wonderfully.

SPINACH BEEF RAVIOLI

The filling for this recipe can be prepared and refrigerated up to 2 days in advance.

Serves 4
30 minutes

2   *cups ground (TVP) beef*
1 ³/₄ *cups beef stock (pg 18)*
1   *bunch fresh spinach (or 10 oz frozen)*
2   *tablespoons olive oil*
1   *medium onion, chopped coarsely*
4   *cloves of garlic, minced*
1 ¹/₂ *teaspoons sea salt*
1   *teaspoon pepper*
1   *tablespoon dried oregano*
4   *tablespoons water*
2   *tablespoons unbleached white flour*
2   *quarts water*
1   *package ravioli or wonton skins**

1. Combine beef and stock in a pot, bring to boil and let sit 10 minutes.

2. Steam the spinach; drain and chop.

3. In a large skillet, heat olive oil. Add onion and garlic; sauté until transparent and lightly browned, about 3 minutes. Add salt, pepper and beef and sauté 3 minutes.

4. In food processor or blender, combine chopped spinach with beef mixture. Blend, but do not puree.

5. Mix 4 tablespoons of water with flour to form a paste that will serve as a "glue."

6. In a large pot, bring 2 quarts of water to boil.

7. Take out ravioli squares one by one. Lay flat on work space and spoon a bit of filling in each center. Brush some flour glue around the edges. Top with another square and press; make sure you squeeze out the air from each pocket. Repeat for remaining ravioli squares.

8. Place in boiling water. Cook for about 2 minutes or until they rise and the dough becomes transparent. Remove gently with slotted spoon.

9. Serve topped with basic tomato sauce (pg 85) or cashew pesto (pg 96).

*Note: Wanton wrappers can be found in the refrigerator section of some supermarkets. Any leftover can be made into crackers by baking 3 minutes at 400° F.

The story goes that pizzas originated in Naples where hungry cooks would tear off dough from bread while it was baking, flatten it and top with whatever savory items were to hand. Tomatoes, so much a part of pizzas today, were not used originally, because they were thought to be poisonous. Cheese only became a part of the pizza scene a century ago, when a chef needed something white for his tomato and basil pizza so as to have all the colors of the Italian flag (red, white and green).

BASIC PIZZA CRUST

Makes about 10 crusts, 10 inches in diameter
1 hour plus 2 hours rising

1	*tablespoon maple syrup*
2	*cups water, warmed*
1	*package yeast*
2	*tablespoons salt*
4	*tablespoons olive oil*
2	*cups whole wheat flour*
6	*cups unbleached flour*
2	*tablespoons gluten flour*
	Garlic butter (pg 23)

1. In a large mixing bowl, combine water and maple syrup; add yeast and let sit 10 – 15 minutes. When it starts to bubble, add salt and oil and slowly work in the flours. Knead until springy, 5 – 10 minutes, occasionally sprinkling more flour to prevent sticking.

2. Place rounded dough in lightly oiled mixing bowl and cover with a damp towel. Set aside in a warm place until doubled in size (about an hour).

3. Remove from bowl, punch down and knead slightly. On a floured surface, roll into a log and cut into nine equal sections. Form each into a ball. Cover with a towel, keep warm, and let rise again for about 45 minutes.

4. Preheat oven and pizza stone (if available) to 500° F.

5. Take a ball of dough and flatten it into a circle by pressing down firmly with the palm of your hand. Then hold the dough in the air and, using your fingers, gently stretch dough around the edge, slowly enlarging the circle shape. Then, with your hands on either side of the diameter, stretch the dough gently while slowly turning the circle; repeat this procedure until you have a circle approximately 10 inches in diameter. Repeat for the other balls of dough.

6. Place pizzas on a cutting board and brush with roasted garlic paste.

7. Place in a heated oven for 3 – 4 minutes until half cooked or until pastry bubbles in parts; these bubbles will turn golden. (Do not wait until the whole crust turns golden—you do not want to fully bake the pizza crust at this point.)

8. Top with your favorite pizza topping or let cool and freeze for use later.

The world's largest pizza was made in Tallahassee, Florida, by Lorenzo Amato in 1991. It was an unbelievable 10,000 square feet in size.

BBQ PIZZA

Why pick a BBQ pizza for topping? Because its unusual, easy and very popular with those who've tried it.

Serves 2
10 minutes plus 20 minutes sauteing/baking

2   tablespoons olive oil
1   medium onion, sliced thinly into rings
1/2 teaspoon sea salt
1/4 teaspoon white pepper
1   tablespoon maple syrup
1   cup beef (seitan) chunks (pp 16 & 18), diced
1/2 cup barbecue sauce
1/2 cup grated, smoked mozzarella (soy) cheese (optional)
1   pizza crust, 10-inch diameter (see above)

1. In a skillet, heat olive oil; add onions and sauté for about 2 minutes until lightly browned and transparent. Add sea salt and pepper, but continue cooking onions on low heat until they become nicely browned and sweetened, about 10 minutes. Add maple syrup and let simmer for 3 to 4 minutes until caramelized.

2. Shred beef chunks into bite size pieces.

3. Mix beef with barbecue sauce.

4. Spread the barbecued beef onto pizza crust and top with caramelized onions; sprinkle with cheese (optional).

5. Preheat oven to 400° F. Bake pizza for about 10 minutes or until cheese has melted.

SCALLOPINI WITH MUSHROOM SAUCE

Serves 4 - 6
20 minutes

6   *four-oz. (tempeh) patties, OR*
6   *thin slices of (seitan) veal (pp 16 & 17)*
2   *tablespoons olive oil*
6   *shallots, sliced*
8   *oz (button) mushrooms, thinly sliced*
$1/2$ *teaspoon sea salt*
1   *tablespoon unbleached, white flour*
$1/2$ *cup (soy) milk*
$1/4$ *cup white cooking wine*
    Sea salt
    Pepper
$1/2$ *cup parsley, finely chopped*

1. Prepare patties according to BLT recipe (pg 51). Cut each into 4 or 5 slices.

2. In a medium skillet, sauté shallots in olive oil until transparent and lightly browned; add mushrooms and $1/2$ teaspoon salt. Sauté 3 minutes until soft.

3. Add flour and stir well for 2 minutes. Stir in soy milk and white wine, bring to simmer and stir until sauce has light, creamy consistency, about 1 minute. Add salt and pepper to taste. Take off heat, and stir in parsley.

4. On serving plate, arrange scallopini slices in fan shape and pour mushroom sauce on top. Serve with rice and vegetables of your choice.

SOPHIA'S SCALLOPINI WITH PORT SAUCE

Serves 4
20 minutes plus overnight marinating (+ sauce time)

4   *quarter-inch thick cuts (seitan) veal (pp 16 & 19)*
³/₄ *cup white wine*
¹/₄ *cup olive oil*
4   *rosemary sprigs*
4   *thyme sprigs*
¹/₄ *cup unbleached flour*
1   *tablespoon salt*
1   *tablespoon pepper*
¹/₄ *cup olive oil*

1. Marinate first five ingredients overnight.
2. Combine flour, salt and pepper and use to coat veal.
3. In a medium skillet, sear in oil to brown both sides and serve straight away with Port sauce.

Port Sauce

Makes 8 cups

¹/₄ *cup olive oil*
1   *cup chopped onion*
4   *garlic cloves, minced*
1   *cup green pepper, chopped*
¹/₂ *cup celery, chopped*
2   *bay leaves*
1   *16-oz can Italian tomatoes, chopped*
1   *6-oz can tomato paste*
1   *16-oz can tomato sauce*
1   *tablespoon salt*
1   *teaspoon pepper*
¹/₄ *cup port*

1. Heat oil in a skillet and sauté onions and garlic until soft, 2 minutes.
2. Add pepper, celery, parsley and bay leaves and sauté 5 minutes.
3. Add remaining ingredients and simmer 30 minutes until reduced.

OSSO BUCCO

A fancy dish to serve on cold nights.

Serves 8
50 minutes plus overnight marinating and 30 minutes simmering

8	*half-inch thick cuts (seitan) veal (pp 16 & 19)*
3/4	*cup white wine*
1/4	*cup olive oil*
4	*rosemary sprigs*
4	*thyme sprigs*
1/4	*cup unbleached flour*
1	*tablespoon salt*
1	*tablespoon pepper*
1/4	*cup olive oil*
2	*yellow onions*
1/2	*teaspoon oregano, dried*
2	*tablespoons basil, dried*
1	*28-oz can whole plum tomatoes, quartered*
1	*teaspoon salt*
1	*teaspoon pepper*
1	*cup white wine*
1	*cup veal stock (pg 19)*
3/4	*cup Italian parsley, chopped*
	Grated zest of 2 lemons
2	*cloves garlic, minced*

1. Marinate first five ingredients overnight.
2. Combine flour, salt and pepper and use to coat veal.
3. In a medium skillet, sear in oil to brown both sides.
4. Remove veal from skillet, add onions, garlic, oregano, half the basil, and sauté ten minutes.
5. Add tomatoes, salt and pepper and simmer 10 minutes.
6. Add wine and stock, bring to boil and simmer 30 minutes to reduce.
7. Add veal to heat for 3 minutes.
8. Sprinkle with parsley, lemon and garlic.
9. Serve with saffron rice and peas, or fettucine, or mashed potatoes.

FRIED CALAMARI

Seitan provides the chewy texture and mild flavor of Calamari.

Serves 4
15 minutes

1/4   cup unbleached flour
1/2   cup (soy) milk
1/4   cup olive oil
1/2   teaspoon salt
1/2   teaspoon black pepper
1   cup bread crumbs, unseasoned
1   teaspoon dried thyme
1/2   cup parsley, finely chopped
4   quarter-inch thick slices (seitan) calamari (pg 16)
1   lemon, cut into 8 wedges

1. Mix flour, milk, 1 tablespoon of oil, salt and pepper to make thin batter.

2. In a separate bowl, mix bread crumbs with thyme and parsley.

3. Dip the calamari slices in the batter and then the bread crumb mixture, ensuring each side is thoroughly coated.

4. In a skillet, heat remainder of oil and fry fillets until brown on both sides, 2–3 minutes each.

5. Serve garnished with lemon wedges.

RISO WITH CASHEW PESTO

Serves 4 - 6
15 minutes

Riso

1   *pound riso/orso pasta*
1   *package (10 oz) frozen peas, lightly defrosted*
1   *cup chopped sausage (pg 20)*
1 ¹/₂ *cups of cashew pesto (below)*

Cashew Pesto

1   *cup olive oil*
1   *cup raw cashew nuts*
¹/₂ *cup grated (soy) parmesan (optional)*
1   *bunch basil*
1   *teaspoon salt (if needed)*
6   *cloves garlic, peeled*
3   *oz pine nuts*

1. In blender, combine all cashew pesto ingredients and process until smooth. This pesto will keep for several weeks if refrigerated.

2. Cook the riso pasta according to package instruction. Drain and return to pot. Add cashew pesto, peas and the chopped sausage. Warm on low heat if needed.

3. Serve with garlic bread.

This pesto is delicious on toast, with baked potatoes, etc. Just watch for garlic breath!

RED CHARD & CHEVRE RAVIOLI

Serves 4
40 minutes

1	_bunch red Swiss chard_
3	_tablespoons olive oil_
1	_medium onion, chopped medium fine_
4	_cloves of garlic, sliced_
1	_teaspoon sea salt_
4	_tablespoons water_
2	_tablespoons unbleached white flour_
2	_quarts of water_
1	_package of ravioli or won-ton skins_
3	_ounces chevre_

1. Wash chard well and remove stems; cut stems and leaves into 1" pieces.

2. In a large skillet, heat olive oil; sauté onion and garlic until lightly browned and transparent; about 2 minutes. Add chard stems and sauté about 2 minutes, then add the leaves and sauté for another 2 – 3 minutes. Add salt, stir well. Take off heat and let cool.

3. Mix 4 tablespoons of water with 2 tablespoons of unbleached white flour to form a paste that will serve as a "glue."

4. In a large pot, bring 2 quarts of water to the boil. Turn down the heat and let simmer while you prepare the ravioli squares.

5. Take out ravioli squares one by one. Lay flat on workspace. Spoon one tablespoon of the chard filling and 1 teaspoon of chevre in the center of each ravioli square. Brush some of the flour glue around the edges. Top with another square and press; make sure you squeeze out the air from each pocket. Repeat for remaining ravioli squares.

6. Place in boiling water. Cook for about 2 minutes or until they rise and the dough becomes transparent. Remove gently with slotted spoon.

7. Serve with red bell pepper sauce (recipe follows).

Note: The filling for this Ravioli can be prepared and refrigerated up to 2 days in advance.

RED BELL PEPPER SAUCE

10 minutes + 45 minutes cooking/cooling
Makes 1 - 2 cups

2   *red bell peppers*
¹/₂   teaspoon sea salt
¹/₂   to 1 cup water

1. Roast or broil bell peppers at 450° - 500° F until charred.
2. Place in a paper bag to cool.
3. Peel off outer skin, remove seeds and stems, chop and place in blender with sea salt and ¹/₂ cup of water.
4. Blend until smooth—add water as necessary.
5. Cover and refrigerate.

This sauce will keep for several days if refrigerated.

CHAPTER SEVEN

Chinese and Other Far East Feasts

With so many people living on a relatively small area of cultivatable land, the Chinese have thoroughly researched the subject of what is edible, as well as cooking techniques to use with scarce energy resources. They have worked at this for several thousand years. The result is almost a reverence for the art of cooking and a cuisine that makes the most of the least. If we are proud of the number of Big Macs served around the world, think how many chow meins have found their way down the hatch.

SWEET & SOUR PORK

Serves 4
30 minutes (not including cooking rice)

2	cups cooked rice (Basmati or your choice)
1	cup pork (TVP) chunks
1	cup beef stock (pg 18)
2	cups of sweet & sour sauce (recipe follows)
1	teaspoon baking powder
1	cup unbleached flour
1 ½	cups soda water
1	teaspoon sea salt
½	cup canola or safflower oil
1	cup snow peas, julienned
2	tablespoons toasted sesame seeds

1. If none in supply, get the rice cooking per package directions.
2. Combine pork with stock in a pan, bring to boil and let sit 10 minutes.
3. Meanwhile, make the sauce, below.
4. Mix baking powder with flour. Whisk in soda water and sea salt until batter reaches a thick, yoghurt-like consistency.

5. Heat oil in heavy skillet while continuing with step 4.

6. Dip pork chunks in soda batter until well coated. Gently place in hot oil. (**Note:** oil must be hot enough to allow chunks to turn crispy quickly without absorbing excess oil.) Fry until golden. Remove and drain on paper towels.

7. Arrange rice in 4 serving dishes. Place pork on top and drizzle with warmed sweet & sour sauce. Garnish with snow peas and toasted sesame seeds.

Sweet & Sour Sauce

Best used immediately, but will keep for several days if refrigerated.

Makes 4 cups

2   *tablespoons miso*
2   *cups unsweetened apple juice*
1   *teaspoon whole grain mustard*
$^1/_2$ *cup maple syrup*
1   *cup water*
$^3/_4$ *cup soy sauce*
$^1/_2$ *cup rice vinegar*
6   *tablespoons cornstarch*

1. Dissolve miso in small amount of water.

2. Combine all ingredients (except cornstarch and 1 cup apple juice) in medium saucepan. Heat until simmering.

3. Dissolve cornstarch in remainder of apple juice.

4. Add cornstarch mixture to saucepan, stirring until sauce thickens and starts to boil. Remove from heat.

You may replace the cornstarch with a product called KUZU or KUDZU, a powder made from the Kuzu plant, originating in Japan (in the Southern United States, Kuzu is considered a noxious weed). Ask for this product in an Asian market or your local healthfood store. If you can get hold of it, try using it as a thickener instead of cornstarch. It is more nutritious and much easier to use (see also note on pg 156).

PORK FRIED RICE

Serves 4
15 minutes (not including rice cooking time)

3   tablespoons vegetable oil
1   medium onion, finely chopped
1   stalk celery, thinly sliced
2   green onions, sliced
1/4 cup green peas
2   cups chopped sausage (pg 20)
3   tablespoons soy sauce
4   cups cooked rice

1. Heat vegetable oil in a large skillet. Add onions and sauté until transparent. Add celery and sauté a minute; add green onions, peas, sausage and soy sauce, stirring well. Continue to cook over medium heat while gradually mixing in rice and salt. Remove from heat and serve.

Any fried rice dish comes out better if you cook the rice the day before—a great way to use leftover rice!

SZECHUAN BEEF

Serves 4
15 minutes plus 20 minutes steaming (not including rice)

4   *cups of cooked or steamed rice of your choice*
1   *cup beef (TVP) chunks*
1   *cup beef stock (pg 18)*
1   *large sweet potato, cut into ¹/₂" slices*
2   *tablespoons vegetable stock*
2   *tablespoons vegetable oil*
1   *tablespoon spicy sesame oil*
¹/₄ *cup brown rice flour, or unbleached white flour*
1   *bunch bok choy*

1. If no rice in supply, get it cooking.
2. Combine beef and stock in a pot, bring to a boil and let sit 10 minutes.
3. Boil the sweet potato for 5 minutes only.
4. Mix the vegetable stock, oils and brown rice flour in a bowl.
5. Toss in the beef chunks, ensure they are well coated.
6. In a steamer tray, place a layer of bok choy leaves on the bottom, then a layer of slightly boiled potatoes; top with beef chunks. Steam for 20 minutes until beef and vegetables are tender.
7. Serve over cooked or steamed rice.

The Chinese have been living off their land for thousands of years, feeding themselves rather than animals. In America, we feed 80% of our corn and 95% of our oats to livestock; we have cleared 260 million acres of forests for croplands to feed animals; and we have lost 75% of our topsoil in 200 years of such practices (85% of which is due to livestock raising). If the Chinese had adopted the same diet and farming practices, they would have become history around 3,000 BC.

CHICKEN CHOW MEIN

Serves 4
40 minutes

1   *ounces dried shiitake mushrooms*
3   *cups chicken stock (pg 19)*
1   *cup chicken (TVP) chunks*
½   *pound Chinese noodles*
6   *tablespoons vegetable oil*
2   *tablespoons toasted sesame oil*
½   *pound bok choy, ½"-slices*
1   *teaspoon salt*
1   *tablespoon soy sauce*
1   *teaspoon cornstarch (or Kuzu), dissolved in*
        2 teaspoons of water
2   *whole green onions, finely chopped*

1. Soak mushrooms in 2 cups boiled stock for 20 minutes and then drain, strain and keep stock for step 6. Remove stems and slice thinly.

2. Combine remaining stock with chicken in another pot, bring to boil and let sit 10 minutes. When cooled, shred with fingers.

3. Bring a large pot of water to boil, gently immerse noodles and cook 3 minutes. Drain, rinse with cold water, then drain again. Return to the pot and mix in 1 tablespoon of vegetable oil.

4. Heat 2 tablespoons vegetable oil in a wok or heavy skillet. Sauté the chicken until lightly brown. Remove and set aside.

5. Heat 3 tablespoons vegetable oil in wok or heavy skillet, add the noodles and stir fry on medium. Without tossing, cook each side about 5 minutes until golden.

6. Heat 2 tablespoons toasted sesame oil in a wok or heavy skillet. Stir fry bok choy for 1 minute. Add chicken, mushrooms, salt, soy sauce and stock. Cook for 3 minutes over high heat. Thicken with dissolved cornstarch.

7. Place noodles on serving plates. Spoon stir fried vegetables & chicken mixture on top. Sprinkle with chopped green onions.

KUNG PAO CHICKEN

In the Szechwan region of China, charred dried chile peppers are eaten along with the chicken. Unless you like very hot food, you will prefer our recipe.

Serves 4
30 minutes (not including rice)

4	*cups of cooked or steamed rice or rice noodles*
$^1/_2$	*cup raw, unsalted peanuts*
1	*cup chicken (TVP) chunks*
1	*cup chicken stock (pg 19)*
3	*tablespoons rice or unbleached flour*
1	*teaspoon salt*
$^1/_2$	*cup (soy) milk*
4	*tablespoons soy sauce*
2	*tablespoon dry sherry or mirin*
2	*tablespoons rice vinegar*
2	*tablespoons maple syrup*
$^1/_4$	*teaspoon red pepper flakes*
1	*teaspoon sesame oil*
1	*teaspoon cornstarch*
$^1/_4$	*cup vegetable oil*
1	*tablespoon hot chili oil**
4 - 6	*small, dry, hot chile peppers*
2	*scallions, cut into $^1/_2$-inch sections*
2	*cloves garlic, chopped fine*

*If you cannot find a hot chile oil, substitute with another oil, preferably a spicy one.

1. If no cooked rice on hand, cook your choice.
2. In a toaster oven, bake peanuts for 12 minutes at 350° until golden.
3. Combine chicken and stock in a pot, bring to boil and let sit 10 minutes.
4. Combine flour, salt, and milk in a bowl and toss chicken in it.
5. In a jar with a lid, combine soy sauce, sherry, vinegar, maple syrup, red pepper flakes, sesame oil and cornstarch and shake to blend.

6. In a wok or sauté pan, heat vegetable oil. Sauté chicken until well browned, about 5 minutes. Remove from heat and set aside.

7. In the wok, add hot chile oil to remnants of vegetable oil. Sauté chile peppers and peanuts and cook, stirring, until peppers just begin to char. If peppers become completely black, discard. Remove peanuts from pan and repeat with new peppers. Remove from pan and set aside.

8. In a wok, quickly sauté scallions and garlic on high heat for about 30 seconds. Turn heat down to medium. Return chicken to wok. Add chile peppers and peanuts. Stir-fry with onions and garlic for about one minute.

9. Add soy sauce mixture and continue to stir fry until chicken is thoroughly coated.

10. Toss in the peanuts and remove from heat.

11. Serve over cooked or steamed rice or rice noodles.

BAKED SPRING ROLLS

These fried pastries are called spring rolls in Shanghai, where the wrapper used makes a delicate crust. The Cantonese use a different wrapper called egg rolls, which give a heavier crust. Both are available in the refrigerator sections of many supermarkets.

Makes 15 rolls
45 minutes plus 20 minutes baking

1   *ounce dried shiitake mushrooms*
1   *cup ground (TVP) beef*
1   *cup beef stock (pg 18)*
4   *tablespoons vegetable oil*
1   *teaspoon ginger, finely chopped*
2   *scallions, finely chopped*
2   *tablespoons soy sauce*
1   *tablespoon maple syrup*
1   *tablespoon sherry or mirin**
2   *tablespoons toasted sesame oil*
$^1/_2$ *Napa cabbage, shredded*
$^1/_2$ *pound bok choy, sliced in $^1/_4$" slices*
1   *carrot, sliced julienne*
$^1/_2$ *stalk celery, thinly sliced*
1   *cup bean sprouts*
1   *teaspoon sea salt*
2   *tablespoons cornstarch (or Kuzu)*
1   *tablespoon water*
20   *egg or spring roll wrappings*

*Mirin is a sweet, low-alcohol, Japanese cooking wine made from rice.

1. Soak mushrooms in boiling hot water for 20 minutes; drain (keep liquid for cooking). Remove stems and slice thinly.
2. Combine ground beef with stock in a pot, bring to boil and let sit 10 minutes.
3. Meanwhile, prepare the vegetables.
4. Heat 2 tablespoons of vegetable oil in a wok or heavy skillet; add ginger and scallions and sauté for 30 seconds. Add ground beef and sauté for another 1 – 2 minutes. Add 1 tablespoon of soy sauce,

maple syrup and sherry; simmer for 1 minute until flavors are fully absorbed. Remove from heat and set aside.

5. Heat toasted sesame oil in wok or heavy skillet. Add cabbage, bok choy, mushrooms, carrots and celery; sauté for 1 minute. Remove from heat, then toss in bean sprouts.

6. Combine ground beef and vegetable mixtures in wok or skillet, adding 1 teaspoon of salt and remainder of the soy sauce. Sauté 3 – 4 minutes. Remove from heat and let cool.

7. Dissolve cornstarch (or Kuzu) in water to make a thick paste that will act as a "glue."

8. Preheat oven to 375° F.

9. On a flat work space, lay out the spring roll wrappers. Spoon about two or three tablespoons of filling in the center of each wrapper. Roll up into envelopes approximately 4" long and 2" wide. Seal wrappers with some cornstarch paste.

10. Brush spring rolls lightly with remainder of vegetable oil. Place rolls in baking pan and bake 15 – 20 minutes until golden and toasty.

11. Serve with Sweet & Sour Sauce (pg 100) or Spicy Mustard Sauce (below).

Spicy Mustard Sauce

(Warning! Hot!)

Makes 2 cups
3 minutes

8   oz whole grain mustard
1   oz wasabi powder (Japanese horseradish powder)
½   cup water

1. In a mixer, combine ingredients and blend well.

If wasabi is hard to find, use 1 cup of regular horseradish instead of the powder and water.

EGG FU YUNG

Serves 4
20 minutes

1   cup unbleached white flour
6   tablespoons vegetable oil
2   teaspoons baking soda
3/4   cup water
1   teaspoon sea salt
1/2   white cabbage, shredded
1   cup grated carrots
1   yellow onion, cut in half, then thinly sliced
2   scallions, finely chopped

1. In a blender or food processor, combine flour, 2 tablespoons of vegetable oil, baking soda, water and salt; blend well until batter reaches a yoghurt-like consistency. Pour into a large bowl.

2. Add cabbage, carrots, onions and half of the chopped scallions to this batter mixture. Stir gently but thoroughly to ensure vegetables are well coated.

3. In a large skillet, heat 1 tablespoon of vegetable oil on medium heat. When hot, gently ladle 2 cups of vegetable mixture into the skillet. Fry 2 minutes until golden; turn over and repeat.

4. Repeat twice more with rest of the mix.

5. Serve drizzled with Teriyaki Glaze (pg 116); garnish with remainder of chopped scallions.

Asian countries have very low rates of heart disease and various cancers. This is in part due to meat and dairy products (when they are included in dishes) traditionally being used sparingly.

CHINESE RICE SALAD

Serves 4
20 minutes (not including rice cooking time)

1   *head Romaine lettuce*
1   *bunch scallions, finely chopped*
1   *cup tomato, finely chopped*
1 ½ *cups fresh (or frozen) corn kernels*
4   *oz cellophane or rice noodles*
½   *cup canola oil*
1   *cup cooked Basmati rice*
1   *cup Sesame Mustard dressing (recipe follows)*
¼   *cup toasted sesame seeds*

1. Clean lettuce and shred into bite size pieces. Clean and chop other vegetables.
2. Heat canola oil in skillet; when sufficiently hot, place a small amount of the noodles in the oil. NOTE: if the oil is hot enough, the noodles will puff up instantly. Fry small amounts at a time until all noodles are done. Drain noodles on a paper towel.
3. In a large bowl, toss lettuce, onions, tomato, corn and Basmati rice.
4. Mix in the Sesame Mustard dressing.
5. Garnish with noodles and toasted sesame seeds.

SESAME MUSTARD DRESSING

Makes 2 cups
5 minutes

1   *3-inch ginger, peeled*
½   *cup untoasted sesame oil*
¼   *cup toasted sesame oil*
¼   *cup Dijon mustard*
½   *cup maple syrup*
½   *cup rice vinegar*

1. Chop ginger in blender and gradually add rest of ingredients until thoroughly blended.

SATAY WITH PEANUT SAUCE

Here's a classic Indonesian dish—Sate with Gado Gado sauce. It has found its way firmly into Dutch cuisine and deserves a place in our kitchens, too.

Serves 4
30 minutes

8	*oz Udon (or plain chinese) noodles*
6	*tablespoons olive oil*
4	*four-oz (tempeh) patties*
1/4	*cup beef stock (pg 18)*
1	*medium onion, sliced thinly*
1	*bunch bok choy, sliced in 1/2" pieces*
1/2	*tsp sea salt*
2	*cups peanut sauce (recipe follows)*
1	*bunch scallions, finely chopped*
1	*cup cilantro leaves*
1	*carrot, shaved (optional)*

1. Cook Udon noodles according to package instructions.

2. Heat 1/4 cup oil in skillet until hot; sauté patties on medium high for 3 – 4 minutes each side, until golden. Pour on stock and let simmer until 1/2 liquid has evaporated. Turn patties and continue to simmer until all liquid has evaporated.

3. Let patties cool, then slice into 1/4" strips. Set aside.

4. Heat 2 tablespoons olive oil in skillet; add onion and sauté until transparent and lightly browned. Add bok choy stems and sauté for one minute, then add leafy parts and sauté another 4 – 5 minutes. Add salt. Remove from heat.

5. Toss vegetable mix with cooked noodles. Arrange on serving dishes. Place pattie strips on top, then drizzle peanut sauce on top. Garnish with chopped scallions and cilantro. Arrange carrot shavings around plate for color.

Udon is a rice noodle. It may be available in the Chinese section of your supermarket or else at a local Asian specialty or health food shop. Try finding the brown rice version, which is more nutritious and has a better flavor.

PEANUT SAUCE

Makes 4 cups
10 minutes

2	*tablespoons olive oil*
$^1/_2$	*onion, chopped medium*
6	*cloves garlic, sliced finely*
$^3/_4$	*cup roasted peanuts*
1	*14-oz can of coconut milk*
$^1/_4$	*cup maple syrup*
$^1/_4$	*cup rice vinegar*
$^1/_4$	*cup soy sauce*
1	*teaspoon red chili flakes*

1. Sauté onion and garlic in oil until transparent.
2. Place onion and garlic mixture in a blender or food processor, together with other ingredients. Blend thoroughly into smooth paste. Serve warm.

Turn this dish into a quick hors d'oeuvre by putting the cooked and sliced patties onto bamboo kebab skewers and serving with warmed peanut sauce.

THAI CHICKEN STIR FRY

Serves 4 - 6
30 minutes

½	*cup chicken (TVP) chunks*
½	*cup chicken stock (pg 19)*
1	*bunch green onions*
3	*tablespoons olive oil*
1	*medium onion, sliced*
6	*garlic cloves, chopped*
	Various stir fry vegetables, sliced Julienne
2	*packages fresh, Yaki Soba "fry" noodles**
1	*cup Yaki Soba sauce (recipe follows)*
4	*tablespoons white rice vinegar*
1	*cup bean sprouts*
1	*cup toasted sesame seeds*

1. Combine chicken with chicken stock, bring to boil and let sit for 10 minutes. When cooled, shred with fingers.

2. Slash the green onions lengthwise and place in iced water until ready to serve, so they will curl.

3. In large stir fry pan, heat olive oil. Add onions and garlic; sauté 2 minutes. Gradually add the other stir fry vegetables and continue to sauté, stirring well, for about 2 minutes.

(NOTE: For larger quantities, it works better to pre-sauté the vegetables in small batches, cooling them quickly and mixing them with the noodles once all vegetables are done.)

4. Add noodles and chicken; continue to sauté until they are heated, about 2 minutes.

5. Add Yaki Soba sauce; continue cooking on low heat until liquid has been absorbed.

6. Take off heat; toss in rice vinegar and bean sprouts.

7. Serve garnished with scallions; sprinkle with toasted sesame seeds.

* Available in refrigerator section of some supermarkets.

YAKI SOBA SAUCE

Makes 4 ¹/₂ cups
5 minutes

1   *3-inch piece of ginger, peeled*
3   *cups beef stock (pg 18)*
¹/₄ *cup maple syrup*
2   *garlic cloves, finely chopped*
¹/₄ *cup soy sauce*
1   *cup rice vinegar*

1. Chop ginger in food processor.
2. Add remaining ingredients and blend thoroughly.

CHICKEN CURRY

What Asian section would be complete without a curry? In America, the word "curry" means any hot-sauced dish from India, deriving from the Indian word "ari," meaning "sauce." But the dried curry powder that we buy to make those sauces today are stereotyped versions of the many types made fresh in India. It may be worth checking out any local Asian market for a greater choice.

Serves 4
20 minutes plus 15 minutes simmering (not including rice)

1	cup jumbo cashew, raw
1	fourteen-oz can coconut milk
1	teaspoon red Thai curry paste
2	tablespoons maple syrup
1	tablespoon soy sauce
1	cup carrots, thinly sliced
1	cup broccoli florets, cut into bite size pieces
1/2	cup Chinese snow peas
1	cup corn kernels (fresh or frozen)
2	cups cooked rice, preferably Basmati
1/2	cup chopped cilantro
2	green onions, finely chopped

0. Make rice if none in supply.

1. Preheat the oven to 375° F.

2. Place cashews on baking sheet and roast 15 minutes, shaking occasionally to ensure done evenly on all sides.

3. In a sauce pan, combine coconut milk, water, Thai curry paste, maple syrup and soy sauce. Mix well to dissolve the curry paste. Add carrots, broccoli, snow peas and corn. Bring to boil and simmer a minute. Remove vegetables, return liquid to simmer and reduce to a thick sauce. Return vegetables to sauce to reheat.

4. Divide cooked rice onto serving dishes. Ladle vegetable mixture over rice. Sprinkle with roasted cashews, freshly chopped cilantro and green onions.

BEEF TERIYAKI

And finally, a dish from Japan.

Serves 4
30 minutes (not including rice)

4   cups cooked or steamed rice of your choice
1   cup beef (TVP) chunks
1   cup beef stock (pg 18)
1   tablespoon vegetable oil
1   teaspoon toasted sesame oil
1   medium onion, sliced in half moons
$^1/_2$ green bell pepper, sliced in thin strips lengthwise
$^1/_2$ red bell pepper, sliced same way
1   stalk celery, thinly sliced
$^1/_2$ teaspoon sea salt
1   cup snow peas, trimmed
$^1/_3$ cup Teriyaki glaze (see below)

1. Cook rice if none in the refrigerator.
2. Combine beef with stock in a pot, bring to boil and let sit 10 minutes.
3. In a large skillet, heat oils to sauté onions until transparent. Add bell peppers, celery and salt, and sauté 2 minutes. Add beef chunks and sauté 2 minutes. Stir in snow peas, add glaze and toss well.
4. Divide the cooked or steamed rice onto four serving dishes. Top with vegetable and beef mixture; serve with extra glaze.

TERIYAKI GLAZE

1   cup water
¹/₂ cup honey
1   lemon, juiced
¹/₃ cup soy sauce
1   1-inch piece ginger, thinly sliced
3   garlic cloves

1. Combine water, honey, lemon juice and soy sauce in a small cooking pot, stirring well until honey dissolves. Add ginger and garlic cloves and bring to the boil. Simmer 5 – 7 minutes.

2. Remove from heat and discard ginger and garlic cloves.

CHAPTER EIGHT

Some Traditional European Cuisine

SHEPHERD'S PIE

Shepherd's Pie is an old and popular dish from the British Isles. It was traditionally made with lamb or mutton, hence the reference to "shepherd." In America, however, the lamb has been replaced by ground beef. This recipe is not a quick one, so reserve it for a weekend evening when it's cold outside and the family could use a warm and hearty meal. If ingredients are hard to come by, then feel free to substitute intelligently.

Serves 8
1 ½ hours and 45 minutes baking

2	cups (seitan) lamb (pg 19)
10	tablespoons olive oil
6	Cipolline onions, peeled and chopped (or 1 sweet onion, or 8 shallots)
14	garlic cloves, chopped
4	cups lamb stock (pg 19)
6	dried shiitake mushrooms
1	onion, chopped
2	teaspoons salt
2	tablespoons (1 teaspoon dried) each of: chopped tarragon, thyme, rosemary, parsley
2	bay leaves
1	cup red wine
1	teaspoon Worcestershire sauce
¼	cup whole wheat flour
2	cups cauliflower florets
2	cups Brussels sprouts

6   *medium potatoes, peeled and quartered*
¹/₃ *cup (soy) milk*
¹/₂ *teaspoon pepper*
2   *tablespoons grated (soy) parmesan (optional)*
12   *Cipolline onions, peeled and quartered*
       (or 1 sweet onion, coarsely chopped, or 12 shallots, halved)
1   *celeriac root peeled, ¹/₄-inch cubes (or 1 cup ¹/₄-inch celery*
       slices)
2   *cups of ¹/₄-inch sliced carrots*
¹/₂ *pound fresh shiitake mushrooms, cleaned, destemmed, bite*
     size

1. Cut lamb into ¹/₄-inch cubes; heat ¹/₄ cup oil in a medium skillet and sauté 6 Cipolline onions, 6 cloves of garlic and seitan. Add ¹/₂ cup stock, reduce heat to low and cook an hour until seitan is slightly crisp outside. Set aside.

2. Bring 1 cup stock to boil in a medium pot and add dried shiitake mushrooms. Leave 20 minutes to rehydrate, then clean grit out of mushrooms. Remove mush-rooms, cut off hard ends of stems and discard; cut mushrooms into small, bite-size pieces; strain and reserve liquid.

3. In large skillet, meanwhile, heat 2 tablespoons oil and sauté onion 5 minutes; add 4 garlic cloves for 2 minutes. Add ¹/₂ teaspoon salt, half of tarragon, rosemary, thyme, parsley, and both bay leaves; cook until onions browned.

4. Add wine and Worcestershire sauce and reduce. Blend in flour and add 2 ¹/₂ cups stock, stirring. Bring to boil and simmer until reduce to about 2 ¹/₂ cups (30 minutes).

5. Bring 4 cups water to boil in the empty mushroom soaking pot, blanche cauliflower ¹/₂ minute and then Brussels 2 minutes, stopping cooking process for each by submerging vegetables in bowl of iced water. Quarter the Brussels.

6. In same water, boil potatoes till done. Add milk, ¹/₂ teaspoon salt, pepper and parmesan and mash till smooth.

7. In a large pot, heat 2 tablespoons oil and sauté onions, celeriac and carrots five minutes. Add mushroom soaking liquid, ¹/₂ teaspoon salt, cover and simmer 5 minutes. Set aside.

8. Pre-heat oven to 375° F.

9. In the skillet the lamb was sauted in, heat 2 tablespoons oil

and sauté fresh mushrooms until softened, 3 minutes, adding 1/2 teaspoon salt.

10. To the large pot, add and heat onion mix, cauliflower, Brussels and dried mushrooms.

11. Add the 2 1/2 cups of sauce, remaining parsley, thyme, tarragon and rosemary; add lamb and bring to simmer.

12. Place meat mix in bottom of casserole dish and spread potatoes on top. Run a fork lightly over potatoes to create shallow furrows.

13. Bake 40-45 minutes uncovered until potatoes browned.

CORNISH PASTIES

Pasties were a savory English turnover the Cornish miner's wives developed for their menfolk to eat for lunch. A convenient way of serving meat and vegetables down in the bowels of the earth, before the days of lunch boxes.

Serves 4
50 minutes plus 45 minutes baking

Gravy

2	*tablespoons olive oil*
1	*onion, chopped*
4	*garlic cloves, chopped*
¹/₂	*teaspoon salt*
1	*tablespoon (¹/₂ teaspoon dried) each of:*
	chopped tarragon, thyme, rosemary, parsley
2	*bay leaves*
1	*cup red wine*
1	*teaspoon Worcestershire sauce*
¹/₄	*cup whole wheat flour*
2	*cups lamb stock (pg 19)*

Filling

1	*cup (TVP) beef chunks*
1	*cup lamb stock (pg 19)*
1	*cup potatoes, ¹/₄" cubes*
¹/₂	*cup carrots, chopped*
¹/₂	*cup thinly sliced leek*
¹/₂	*cup celery, chopped*
3	*tablespoons parsley, minced*
¹/₂	*teaspoon salt*
¹/₄	*teaspoon pepper*
¹/₄	*teaspoon cayenne*

Pastry

3/4   *cup mushroom stock*
4   *tablespoons arrowroot*
2   *tablespoons olive oil*
2   *cups whole wheat pastry flour*
1/2   *cup unbleached flour*
1   *teaspoon salt*
    Olive oil spray

1. Combine beef chunks and 1 cup stock in a saucepan, bring to boil and let sit 10 minutes to reconstitute.

2. In medium skillet, heat oil and sauté onions 5 minutes; add garlic and seasoning and cook until onions browned, 10 minutes.

3. Add wine and Worcestershire sauce and simmer 10 minutes.

4. Blend in flour, then add stock, stirring to boil.

5. Simmer 15 minutes, stirring occasionally, until reduced to gravy consistency. Remove bay leaves.

6. Meanwhile, prepare and combine ingredients for filling. Add gravy when done.

7. Preheat oven to 425° F.

8. Add arrowroot to stock and oil in a jar and shake.

9. Mix flour and salt, pour stock into flour and work into a ball.

10. Divide into 4 and roll into 9-inch circles, 1/8-inch thick. Refrigerate until filling ready.

11. Place quarter of filling on each pastry, fold in half and seal by pressing with the tines of a fork; trim edges and make an air hole in each.

12. Place on a cookie tray and bake 15 minutes; reduce to 350° for further 30 minutes, until golden. Spray with olive oil last 5 minutes.

13. Serve hot or cold.

PORK CUTLETS WITH 40 GARLIC CLOVES

Although most countries of the world have a tradition of garlic in the kitchen (the exceptions are England, Scandinavian countries and Japan), none are quite as serious garlicophiles as the French. 40 cloves is apparently the National Recommended Daily Allowance.

Serves 4
15 minutes plus 30 minutes baking

2   *tablespoons olive oil*
4   *shallots, sliced thinly*
1   *pound of (seitan) pork (pp 16 & 19), cut into ¹/₂" slices*
¹/₂ *cup beef stock (pg 18)*
40   *garlic cloves*
¹/₂ *teaspoon salt*
¹/₂ *teaspoon black pepper*
¹/₂ *teaspoon red chili flakes*
     Olive oil spray

1. Preheat oven to 375° F.
2. In an ovenproof casserole dish, heat half the oil; sauté shallots 2 minutes.
3. Add pork slices and sauté 3 minutes until browned; turn and sauté the other side until brown, 2 minutes.
4. Add beef stock and simmer until most of the liquid has evaporated, about 3 minutes. Remove from heat.
5. Sprinkle garlic, salt, pepper and chile flakes evenly over pork. Spray with oil.
6. Bake uncovered 25 minutes, spraying from time to time. The garlic should be nicely browned, but not crunchy.

There are a few tricks of the trade in using garlic: choose only bulbs that are firm, without wrinkling or browning. If the bulbs sprout, then remove the green germs, which are bitter. Use garlic as soon as it is cut to avoid losing its flavor through rapid oxidization. Overheating garlic will make it bitter.

FRENCH ONION SOUP

Serves 4
15 minutes and 35 minutes simmering

¹/₄	cup olive oil
4	medium onions, sliced into thin rings or half moons
5	cloves garlic, thinly sliced
1	teaspoon sea salt
6	cups beef stock (pg 18)
1	cup red wine
2	teaspoons black pepper
¹/₂	French bread (baguette)
	Garlic butter (pg 23)
¹/₂	cup grated Parmesan (soy) cheese (optional)

1. Heat olive oil in large soup pot; add onions and garlic and sauté 4 minutes until transparent. Add salt and heat on low about 15 minutes until the onions are browned.

2. Add the stock and red wine. Bring to boil and simmer for about 20 minutes. Season with black pepper.

3. Cut baguette into ¹/₂" slices. Brush garlic butter on each slice (one side only). Sprinkle with parmesan and toast in broiler or toaster oven for several minutes until done.

4. Ladle soup in serving cups or bowls. Top with the toasted bread.

PÂTÉ MAISON

To make a country style pâté, leave the mixture fairly chunky.

Makes 2 cups
25 minutes

4	*four-oz (tempeh) patties*
¼	*cup olive oil (or olive oil spray)*
½	*cup beef stock (pg 18)*
2	*bunches green onions, sliced*
½	*cup dill*
1	*cup Nayonaise®*
1	*teaspoon sea salt*

1. Preheat grill.

2. Heat oil in a skillet until hot; sauté patties on medium high until each side is golden (4 minutes). Pour on stock and simmer until liquid has almost evaporated. Turn the patties over and continue to simmer until all liquid has evaporated. Transfer to grill and heat 5 minutes each side. Let cool slightly.

3. Combine patties with other ingredients in a food processor and pulse until all items are well blended.

Variation

Sauté and add 4 cups sliced mushrooms to the food processor for a "Pâté Champignon."

PAELLA

Paella is a Spanish dish named after the large skillet it was customarily cooked in over an outdoor, wooden fire. It is a stew similar to the Cajun Jambalaya, consisting of rice flavored with poultry, meat, seafood—whatever is to hand, and some vegetables thrown in toward the end.

Serves 4
25 minutes plus 40 minutes simmering/baking (not including sausage)

2	cups chopped sausage (pg 20)
	Pinch saffron
4	cups chicken stock (pg 19)
1/4	cup olive oil
1	Spanish onion, finely chopped
4	garlic cloves, sliced fine
2	cups rice
2	4-oz chicken (tempeh) fillets
1	teaspoon dry oregano
1 1/2	cups fresh or frozen peas
1	cup corn kernels (fresh or frozen)
1	cup green bell pepper, cut into thin strips
1	cup red bell pepper, cut into thin strips

1. If none in supply, make sausage.
2. Soak saffron in 2 tablespoons of chicken stock.
3. In a large sauté pan, heat half the oil and sauté onions and garlic 3 minutes.
4. Stir in rice and saffron and sauté 5 minutes. Add all but 1/4 cup of stock, bring to boil, cover and simmer 20 minutes.
5. In another sauté pan, heat remaining oil and sauté chicken fillets 4 minutes each side until golden. Slice each into 4 strips.
6. Preheat oven to 350° F.
7. Mix remaining stock and oregano, pour over chicken strips and let liquid be absorbed into both sides.
8. In a shallow casserole dish, combine the rice mix, chicken strips, sausage, peas, corn, and bell pepper strips.
9. Cover and bake 30 minutes.

SHISH KEBAB

Otherwise known as barbecued brochettes, this delicacy comes to us courtesy of the eastern Mediterranean.

Serves 6
45 minutes

2	*cups large (TVP) beef chunks*
1 1/2	*cups beef stock (pg 18)*
2	*tablespoons olive oil*
1	*onion, chopped*
4	*cloves garlic, sliced fine*
1/2	*cup rice vinegar*
1/2	*cup maple syrup*
1	*red bell pepper, sliced lengthwise & cut into squares*
1	*red onion, sliced into thick, half moons*
2	*cups mushrooms, destemmed*
2	*yellow summer squash, sliced 1/4" thick*
2	*green summer squash, sliced 1/4" thick*
1	*basket cherry tomatoes*
1	*package bamboo skewers*
	Olive oil spray

1. Combine stock and beef, bring to boil and let sit 10 minutes.
2. Heat oil in sauté pan, add onions and garlic, and sauté 3 minutes.
3. Add beef chunks, vinegar and syrup, bring to boil and simmer until liquid reduced to a glaze minutes.
4. Preheat grill.
5. Skewer meat and vegetables.
6. Spray with olive oil.
7. Grill about 7 minutes, turning brochettes occasionally to ensure all sides are evenly cooked.

The European Economic Community's response to the routine feeding of antibiotics to livestock was to ban the practice because infections in humans who ate those meats became resistant to antibiotics. The US meat and pharmaceutical industries completely support the use of antibiotics for livestock. Now why would these two industries do something like that?

MOUSSAKAS

This Greek favorite has many variations. It can be made the day before serving; like so many of us, it improves with age. It also freezes well.

Serves 6
30 minutes plus 2 ½ hours baking

2	medium eggplants
3	teaspoons sea salt
1	cup ground (TVP) beef
1	cup beef stock (pg 18)
2	tablespoons olive oil
1	onion, finely chopped
2	twenty-eight oz cans chopped tomatoes
3	teaspoons dried oregano
1	teaspoon black pepper
	Olive oil spray
2	medium potatoes, cut in ¼" slices
3	medium zucchinis, cut lengthwise in ¼" slices

1. Slice eggplants lengthwise ¼" thick. Sprinkle with ½ teaspoon salt; let sit 10 minutes. Turn over and lay on a paper towel, allowing liquid to "sweat" out of eggplant. Repeat procedure for other side.

2. Combine beef and water in a small pan, bring to boil and let sit 10 minutes.

3. Preheat oven to 375° F.

4. In sauté pan, heat oil and sauté onion 3 minutes. Stir in beef and tomatoes. Add oregano, remainder of salt and pepper and simmer 15 minutes.

5. Spray an 8x13 baking dish, layer potatoes at the bottom and cover them with tomato sauce; add a layer of eggplant slices and then more tomato sauce; add a layer of zucchini slices and top with remaining tomato sauce.

6. Cover baking dish with aluminum foil and bake approximately 2 ½ hours until vegetables are well cooked.

CABBAGE ROLLS

Serves 6
30 minutes plus 2 ¹/₂ hours simmering/baking

1	*white cabbage, destemmed*
1	*cup ground (TVP) beef*
1	*cup beef stock (pg 18)*
2	*tablespoons olive oil*
1	*onion, chopped*
3	*garlic cloves, chopped*
³/₄	*cup uncooked short grain brown rice (e.g. Basmati)*
¹/₂	*cup finely chopped parsley*
1	*can (14 oz) chopped tomatoes*
1	*teaspoon sea salt*
¹/₂	*teaspoon pepper*
1	*can (16 oz) tomato sauce*
1	*tablespoon maple syrup*
1	*tablespoon garlic butter*

1. Steam whole cabbages in 1" water until tender; 15 - 20 minutes, depending on size. Let cool.

2. Combine beef and stock in a pan, bring to boil and let sit 10 minutes.

3. Sauté onions and garlic in 2 tablespoons of olive oil until lightly browned and transparent, about 2 minutes. Add ground beef, sauté for another minute. Gradually add rice, parsley, tomatoes, sea salt and pepper. Simmer about 10 minutes until flavors are fully absorbed.

4. Preheat oven to 350° F.

5. Separate cabbage leaves.

6. Spoon some filling onto each cabbage leaf (you may combine several leaves to help make a stronger wrapper); roll into small logs.

7. Lightly oil a 14x8 baking pan and add 1 cup of water. Place cabbage logs in baking pan. Cover with foil and bake for 2 hours until rice is fully cooked.

8. Thoroughly blend tomato paste, maple syrup and garlic butter; add salt and pepper to taste.

9. Serve cabbage rolls topped with the warmed tomato sauce and lemon potatoes below.

LEMON POTATOES

Serves 6
10 minutes plus 30 minutes cooking

3   *large potatoes (Yukon Gold), scrubbed but unpeeled*
2   *tablespoons garlic butter (pg 23)*
    Juice of ½ lemon
2   *tablespoons parsley, chopped fine*
½   *small onion, chopped fine*

1. Boil potatoes and cut into 3/4" cubes.
2. Combine garlic oil, lemon juice, parsley and chopped onion; mix thoroughly.
3. Toss potatoes with mix.

On one acre of land, a farmer can produce either 20,000 pounds of potatoes or 165 pounds of beef. If Americans reduced their consumption of meat by a mere 10% and farmers produced vegetables and grains instead which were then distributed properly, the 20 million people who are dying each year around the world of starvation could be fed properly, and there would still be enough food remaining to feed an additional 40 million people.

WIENER SCHNITZEL WITH GERMAN POTATOES

Serves 4
25 minutes

5   *tablespoon olive oil*
2   *cups (soy) milk*
2   *teaspoons salt*
1   *teaspoon pepper*
4   *four-oz (tempeh) patties*
²/₃   *cup bread crumbs, unseasoned*
¹/₂   *cup chopped parsley*

1. Combine 2 tablespoons oil, milk, half salt and pepper. Marinate patties in this mixture 15 minutes.
2. Combine bread crumbs, remaining salt and parsley and mix.
3. Remove patties and dip in bread crumbs until evenly coated on both sides.
4. Heat remaining oil and sauté patties 3 minutes per side until brown.
5. Serve with cranberry or lingenberry sauce, or chutney.

Variation

Baking gives a crispier crust and reduces oil required:

1. Preheat oven to 375° F if baking.
2. Place coated patties on lightly oiled baking sheet.
3. Bake 20 minutes; turn and bake another 20 minutes.

GERMAN POTATOES

Serves 4
10 minutes and 10 - 20 minutes boiling

1	*pound potatoes*
1	*tablespoon olive oil*
¹/₄	*cup parsley, finely chopped*
¹/₄	*bunch chives, finely chopped*
¹/₄	*teaspoon sea salt*

1. Boil whole potatoes 10 – 20 minutes, depending on their size. Do not overcook. If the potatoes are large, cut into halves or quarters and remove the skin.

3. Mix olive oil, parsley, chives and sea salt.

4. Toss potatoes with this mixture and serve warm.

If you can, find baby red or white roast potatoes. If these are not available, look for a firm boiling potato (as opposed to a baking potato). If new harvest potatoes are available, get them—they are the most nutritious and flavorful.

SAUERBRATEN

"Sauerbraten" means "sour roast," and refers to the marinating of the beef in vinegar, wine and herbs for days. In Germany, beef used to come from cows that were too old for milking. The meat was tough and the marinating process made it tender and gave it some flavor. In this recipe, the marinade process is still done, not because we need to tenderize old cow carcasses, but because the marinade flavors need to mature and seep into the "meat." The recipe therefore needs to be started a day ahead.

Serves 4
30 minutes plus a day marinating and simmering

1	pound of (seitan) beef (pp 16 & 18)
$^1/_2$	teaspoon peppercorns
4	bay leaves
8	whole cloves
$^1/_2$	cup red wine vinegar
1 $^1/_2$	cups water
$^1/_4$	cup olive oil
2	medium onions, sliced
1	small carrot, minced
1	stalk celery, chopped

1. Place beef and seasonings in a deep dish.
2. Bring vinegar and water to boil and pour over meat. When cooled, cover and refrigerate for a day.
3. When ready to cook, remove meat from marinade, heat oil in a Dutch oven and brown beef and vegetables. Remove vegetables.
4. Strain marinade and pour over meat. Bring to boil, cover and simmer slowly for half an hour. Remove lid and reduce liquid. When almost a gravy consistency, add vegetables and reduce to gravy consistency.
5. Serve with braised red cabbage.

BRAISED RED CABBAGE

Serves 4 - 6
15 minutes, plus 30 baking

¹/₄	*cup olive oil*
2	*medium Spanish onions, chopped coarsely*
1	*teaspoon sea salt*
¹/₂	*red cabbage, thinly sliced*
1	*teaspoon caraway seeds*
¹/₃	*cup red wine vinegar*
2	*cups unsweetened apple juice*

1. Preheat oven to 350° F.

2. Heat oil in medium skillet; add onions and sauté 3 minutes. Add salt and cabbage; sauté for 3 minutes, stirring to mix. Stir in caraway seeds, vinegar and apple juice, and bring to simmer.

3. Place cabbage mixture in a baking pan, cover with foil and bake 30 minutes.

SPICY HUNGARIAN GOULASH

For the beef, we recommend Heartline's chunky chicken TVP product—it has an excellent texture for beef!

Serves 4
20 minutes plus one hour in oven

2   *cups beef (seitan or TVP) chunks (pp 16 & 18)*
1   *cup chicken stock (pg 19)*
1   *cup red wine*
2   *tablespoons olive oil*
1   *medium onion, coarsely chopped*
4   *garlic cloves, sliced finely*
1   *teaspoon sea salt*
$^1/_2$ *teaspoon black pepper*
1   *red bell pepper, thinly sliced*
1   *green bell pepper, thinly sliced*
1   *yellow bell pepper, thinly sliced*
$^1/_2$ *teaspoon crushed red chile flakes*
4   *cups basic tomato sauce (pg 85)*
2   *teaspoons oregano*
1   *cup fresh basil, chopped*

1. If using TVP chunks, combine with wine and stock in a pan, bring to boil, and let sit 10 minutes to reconstitute.

2. Preheat oven to 350°.

3. In a large roasting pan, sauté onions and garlic in oil until transparent and lightly browned, about 3 minutes. Add salt, pepper and beef and sauté 3 minutes. Add bell peppers, crushed red chiles and oregano; sauté another 3 minutes. Add tomato sauce, red wine and basil, stir well and bring to simmer.

4. Cover and bake for 1 hour.

5. Serve with pasta of your choice.

CHICKEN PAPRIKA (or Paprikash)

The traditional accompaniment to Paprikash in Hungary is home made "nockerln" (dumplings), but noodles, pasta or rice work equally well. "Paprika" is the Hungarian word for "pepper." Sweet Paprika is ground from peppers that have had their hot seeds removed.

Serves 4
25 minutes

½	cup olive oil
4	four-oz chicken (tempeh) fillets
4	medium onions, finely chopped
6	tablespoons Hungarian sweet paprika
2	teaspoons sea salt
1	teaspoon black pepper
3	cups (soy) milk
1	cup rice OR
1	pound noodles or pasta

1. If having rice, cook it per package directions.

2. In a large saucepan, heat half oil and sauté fillets 4 minutes each side until both sides are golden. Cut each into 1" slices.

3. If having pasta, cook it per package directions.

4. In same pan, sauté onions 3 minutes. Add paprika and sauté 2 minutes.

5. Stir in milk, salt and pepper. Add chicken strips, bring to boil and simmer 10 minutes.

6. Serve the Chicken Paprika over cooked rice or pasta.

BEEF STROGANOFF

Serves 4
20 minutes

2   *cups beef stock (pg 18)*
1   *cup beef (TVP) chunks*
1   *lb fettucine pasta*
¹/₄ *cup olive oil*
1   *onion, finely chopped*
8   *oz mushrooms, sliced*
2   *tablespoons unbleached flour*
1   *cup (soy) milk*
1   *teaspoon Dijon mustard*
¹/₄ *teaspoon pepper*
¹/₂ *teaspoon salt*
¹/₂ *lemon juiced*
1   *cup soft tofu*

1. Combine beef and half stock in a pot, bring to boil and let sit 10 minutes.

2. Boil water for pasta and cook pasta per directions.

3. Heat half oil in skillet, add onion and sauté 3 minutes. Set aside and sauté mushrooms in remaining oil 3 minutes. Add onions and beef and sauté one minute.

4. Sprinkle with flour and stir until absorbed. Mix in remaining stock slowly, stirring 3 – 5 minutes until thickened.

5. Stir in milk, mustard and pepper and simmer until thickened, about 10 minutes. Remove from heat.

6. In a bowl, whisk lemon and salt into tofu to make sour cream and stir into the stroganoff.

7. Place fettucine on plate and top with stroganoff.

IVAR
(Eggplant Dip)

Makes 6 cups
45 minutes

2   *large eggplants*
3   *red bell peppers*
6   *cloves garlic, finely chopped*
$^1/_2$ *cup olive oil*
$^1/_4$ *cup white wine vinegar*
1   *teaspoon sea salt*

1. Roast eggplant and peppers in broiler until blistered. Turn from time to time to ensure all sides are done. Be careful not to burn.

2. Place in paper bag and let them cool down.

3. Peel skins; remove seeds & stems from bell peppers.

4. Combine garlic, oil, eggplant and bell peppers in a blender or food processor. Puree. Blend in vinegar and salt.

5. Serve with herbed pita wedges (below), your favorite crackers or slices of warmed French bread.

Variation

Add 1 tablespoon of freshly chopped yellow chile or 1 teaspoon of crushed red chile flakes to give this Ivar dip a kick!

HERBED PITA WEDGES

Makes 30 - 40 wedges
10 minutes plus 10 minutes baking

3   tablespoons olive oil
3   tablespoons fresh basil, minced
¹/₂   teaspoon kosher (large grain) salt
5   large pita pockets (preferably wholeweat)

1. Preheat oven to 450° F.
2. Combine olive oil, basil and salt in a bowl; mix well.
3. Cut pita pockets into 6 or 8 wedges each.
4. Toss pita wedges in olive oil mixture until evenly coated on both sides.
5. Place pita wedges on baking sheets in single layers. Bake at 450° F for 4 minutes, turn over and bake 4 minutes until golden. They will be crisp when cooled.

These pita crisps can be made up to 2 days in advance. When they have cooled, store them in an airtight container. If needed, recrisp by placing in a preheated oven at 400° F for 2 minutes.

CHAPTER NINE

Breaking the Fast

FRENCH TOAST

The French call their French toast, "pain perdu," meaning "lost bread." It is made using stale bread which might otherwise go to waste—the same rationale, surely, for England's Bread and Butter Pudding. Your French toast (and stale bread!) will no doubt taste better by following this tradition.

Serves 4
15 minutes

¹/₂	*ripe banana*
1 ¹/₂	*cups (soy) milk*
2	*teaspoons vanilla*
4	*tablespoons maple syrup*
3	*teaspoons cinnamon*
¹/₄	*teaspoon salt*
	Grated zest of 1 orange
8	*slices (whole grain) bread*
	Canola oil spray
	Maple syrup

1. Preheat griddle to 375°.
2. Puree first 7 ingredients in blender.
3. Place mix in a wide-bottomed bowl and immerse bread very briefly.
4. Grill 2 – 3 minutes each side on oiled griddle, until lightly browned.

> **In making crepes, blintzes and pancakes, let the mix sit so the ingredients can develop properly. Cook on medium for 1 to 2 minutes on each side, the second side requiring less time. Crepes and blintzes should be turned when the edges appear cooked, as they are very thin. For thicker pancakes, however, wait until the bubbles on the upper surface burst.**

STRAWBERRY BLINTZ

Technically, the difference between a blintz and a crepe is that the blintz is cooked only on one side, then filled and fried just before serving. As you can see, our blintz probably qualifies as a crepe, but who's counting? This is the blintz recipe that Tanya was taught by her mother, so a blintz it is.

Makes 8 blintzes
35 minutes

2 ¼ cups water
1 ¾ cups unbleached white flour
     Canola spray
1   *teaspoon sea salt*

1. Whisk water, salt and flour into a thin batter.
2. Heat on medium and spray very lightly a 9-inch skillet. Pour ⅓ cup batter in skillet and cook about 2 minutes each side until golden.
3. Repeat procedure for remainder of batter. Stack crepes on a warm plate until all are done.
4. Serve with strawberry filling.

STRAWBERRY FILLING

Makes 2 cups

2   *baskets fresh strawberries*
¹/₄   *cup unsweetened apple juice*
3   *tablespoons maple syrup*

1. Remove stems from strawberries; mash half the berries and place in a small saucepan with apple juice. Bring to the boil and simmer 5 minutes until strawberries are lightly cooked and soft.

2. Meanwhile, destem and slice remaining strawberries and place in medium bowl.

3. Combine cooked strawberries with maple syrup in a blender and puree.

4. Add cooked mix to strawberry slices and mix in gently.

5. Serve with blintzes or other pancakes or waffles.

BANANA PANCAKES

Makes 8 pancakes
20 minutes

2 ¼ *cups water*
1 ¼ *cups unbleached white flour*
½   *cup whole wheat pastry flour*
1   *teaspoon sea salt*
     Canola spray
1   *cup coconut milk*
⅓   *cup maple syrup*
3   *ripe bananas, thinly sliced*

1. Whisk water, salt and flour together to make a thin batter.

2. Heat on medium and lightly spray a 9-inch skillet. Pour ⅓ cup batter into skillet; cook 1 – 2 minutes on each side until golden.

3. Repeat for remainder of batter. Stack crepes on a warm plate until all are done.

4. Combine coconut milk and maple syrup, whisking thoroughly.

5. Roll sliced bananas into the warm crepes and drizzle with the coconut & maple syrup.

In buying maple syrup, don't even bother with the sugar and water mixes at the supermarket. Go for the real maple syrup that comes from maple trees. Grade A is the lightest and mildest, while Grade B has the stronger flavor and darker color. Try to obtain organic syrup, as there is no evidence that the paraformaldehyde pellets used by some harvesters actually preserve you.

FOUR GRAIN PANCAKES

Makes 8 pancakes
20 minutes

1	cup unbleached flour
1/4	cup buckwheat flour *
1/4	cup corn meal
1/4	cup millet
2	teaspoons baking powder
2	teaspoons salt
1	cup water
1	cup (soy) milk
	Canola oil spray
	Maple syrup

1. Combine the flours, baking powder and salt. Gradually whisk in water and soy.

2. Heat on medium and lightly oil a 9-inch skillet and pour in 1/3 cup batter. Cook about 1 minute on each side until golden.

3. Repeat for rest of batter, stacking pancakes on a warm plate until all are done.

4. Serve with maple syrup or your favorite topping.

*Try substituting different flours such as rye, oats and spelt.

Pancakes, griddlecakes and hoecakes are all the same water and flour mix. The different names originate from the different types of heating surfaces the pioneers used when they made them.

CORN PANCAKES

Makes 8 pancakes
45 minutes

1   *red bell pepper*
¹/₂   *cup cornmeal*
1   *cup unbleached white flour*
¹/₂   *cup wholewheat pastry flour*
2   *teaspoons baking powder*
1   *teaspoons salt*
2 ¹/₂ cups water
2   *tablespoons canola oil*
    Canola oil spray

1. Roast bell pepper until blistered on all sides (do not burn). Put in paper bag to cool. Peel and remove stems and seeds. Chop finely.
2. Combine flours, baking powder and salt. Gradually whisk in water and oil. Stir in chopped bell peppers.
3. Heat a 6-inch skillet on medium and spray lightly with oil. Pour in ¹/₃ cup of batter and cook 2 minutes each side until golden.
4. Repeat for remaining batter, stacking pancakes on a warm plate.
5. Serve with fresh corn salsa (pg 55 & 56).

SCRAMBLED EGGS

Its not clear who invented scrambled eggs, but they were popularized as a breakfast dish in Victorian England.

Serves 4
15 minutes plus 10 minutes draining

1   _pound firm tofu_
       Olive oil spray
1   _onion, finely chopped_
$^1/_2$ _red bell pepper, finely chopped_
$^1/_2$ _teaspoon tumeric_
1 $^1/_2$ _teaspoons sea salt_

1. Drain excess water from tofu. Let stand for 15 minutes and drain again.
2. Heat olive oil in skillet or sauté pan. Add onions and sauté until lightly browned and transparent, about 2 minutes. Add bell pepper and sauté another 2 – 3 minutes. Crumble tofu over the vegetables, add tumeric and salt. Simmer 4 – 5 minutes, stirring occasionally, until flavors are fully absorbed.

EGGS FLORENTINE

Serves 8
30 minutes

2	*pounds fresh (or 20 oz frozen) spinach*
¹/₂	*cup water*
2	*tablespoons olive oil*
1 ¹/₄	*teaspoons tumeric*
20	*oz extra firm tofu, cut into ¹/₂" slices*
4	*shallots, thinly sliced*
2	*cups (soy) milk*
2	*tablespoons arrowroot or kuzu*
1	*teaspoon salt*
¹/₂	*teaspoon white pepper*
¹/₄	*cup fresh squeezed lemon juice*
3	*tablespoons parsley, chopped*
2	*tomatoes, sliced thick*
8	*English muffins*

1. In a large cooking pot, steam the washed spinach in ¹/₂ cup water until wilted and soft, about 5 minutes. Drain in colander, squeezing out any excess moisture. Chop finely. Set aside.

2. In a sauté pan, heat olive oil. Stir one teaspoon of tumeric into the oil while it is heating. Place tofu slices in hot oil and allow to brown, about 2 minutes on each side.

3. Remove tofu from pan and drain on paper towel.

4. Sauté shallots in oil remaining in pan for 3 minutes.

5. Mix kuzu, salt and white pepper into soy milk and stir until arrowroot/kuzu dissolve. Add this mixture to shallots in sauté pan. Heat until sauce begins to thicken. Allow to cool slightly. Pour mixture into food processor or blender. Add lemon juice and remainder of tumeric and puree.

6. Separate English muffins into halves and toast lightly.

7. On each half, place two slices of tofu, top with some spinach and a slice of tomato, then drizzle with sauce. Serve garnished with parsley.

An Italian princess from the town of Florence married the King of France almost five hundred years ago. She must have felt the French cuisine at the time needed some pizazz, as she brought her chefs with her. Florence was obviously surrounded by fields of spinach at that time, because the chefs were in the habit of adding it to many dishes. The term "Florentine" in cooking, therefore, came to mean a dish made "on a bed of spinach." Presumably, the princess' bed was made of something else.

BREAKFAST POTATOES

Serves 4
15 minutes plus 15 minutes sauteing

1	_pound potatoes (Yukon Gold or White Rose)_
	Olive oil spray
2	_onions, sliced_
4	_cloves garlic, sliced_
2	_teaspoons dried thyme_
$1/2$	_teaspoon sea salt_
$1/4$	_teaspoon black pepper_

1. Cube potatoes and place in boiling water. Boil until fork tender.

2. Heat large skillet, spray liberally with oil and sauté onions and garlic for 2 minutes. Add potatoes, thyme, salt and pepper and cook on medium low until potatoes are golden, about 15 minutes. Stir occasionally to prevent burning.

3. Serve with chopped breakfast sausage (pg 20) and scrambled eggs (pg 145).

OATMEAL & RAISIN MUFFIN

Makes 8 large muffins
15 minutes plus 25 minutes baking

1 ¹/₂ cups wholewheat pastry flour
¹/₂   cup unbleached flour
1   tablespoon baking powder
¹/₄   teaspoon sea salt
¹/₂   teaspoon cinnamon
¹/₂   teaspoon ground cardamon
1   cup oatmeal
¹/₂   cup raisins
²/₃   cup (soy) milk
¹/₂   cup canola oil
5   oz soft tofu
¹/₂   cup maple syrup
1   teaspoon vanilla extract
*   Spray butter*

1. Preheat oven to 375° F.
2. Sift flours, baking powder, salt, cinnamon and cardamon in a large bowl.
3. Add oatmeal and raisins, mixing thoroughly.
4. In blender or food processor, puree liquid ingredients.
5. Pour liquid into flours and mix thoroughly.
6. Lightly grease a muffin tin with spray butter.
7. Pour dough into muffin tin, filling each hole almost to the top.
8. Bake 25 minutes or until golden.

BLUEBERRY MUFFINS

Makes 8 large muffins
15 minutes plus 35 minutes baking

1   *cup of blueberries, fresh or frozen*
½   *cup unbleached flour*
2 ½ *cups wholewheat pastry flour*
1   *tablespoon baking powder*
⅔   *cup (soy) milk*
¼   *cup canola oil*
5   *oz soft tofu*
½   *cup maple syrup*
1   *teaspoon vanilla extract OR*
¼   *teaspoon almond extract*

1. Toss blueberries in ¼ cup of unbleached flour.
2. In a bowl, mix flours with baking powder and add blueberries.
3. Puree remaining ingredients in a blender/food processor.
4. Pour liquid into flours and mix thoroughly.
5. Lightly grease a muffin tin with spray butter.
6. Pour dough into muffin tin, filling each hole almost to the top.
7. Bake 35 minutes or until golden.

CINNAMON ROLLS

Makes a dozen rolls
40 minutes plus 3 ½ hours rising, baking

2	*envelopes yeast*
½	*cup warm water*
1	*cup amasake or soy milk, warmed*
¼	*cup Fruitsource® (see note) or maple syrup*
4	*tablespoons canola oil*
1	*teaspoon sea salt*
4 ½	*cups whole wheat pastry flour*
¼	*cup gluten flour*
	Canola spray
2	*teaspoons cinnamon*
¼	*teaspoon cloves, ground*
1	*cup chopped pecans*
½	*cup FruitSource® sugar*
1	*teaspoon orange rind*
¼	*cup plumped raisins*
1	*ripe banana*
1	*cup cream (pg 153), optional*

1. Dissolve yeast in water and add milk, syrup, 2 tablespoons oil, and salt; let sit 10 minutes until bubbles.

2. Work in flours and knead 5 – 10 minutes until smooth and elastic.

3. Grease large bowl with oil spray, and place dough in it. Cover with damp towel and let rise in warm area for 1 ½ hours till doubled in size.

4. Punch down and repeat for half an hour.

5. Mix spices, nuts, fruits, sugar and dried fruits.

6. Mash banana and combine with last 2 tablespoons of oil.

7. When doubled in size, roll dough into 15x7 rectangle.

8. Spread banana mix over dough and sprinkle nut mix evenly over rectangle.

9. Tightly roll up the long side of the dough and pinch edges to seal.

10. Stretch the "sausage" to flatten any bulges and slice into 1-inch pieces.

11. Place slightly apart in a greased, high-sided 13x9 inch baking pan.

12. Cover with a damp cloth and return to a warm area for 40 minutes until doubled in size.

13. Preheat oven to 375° and bake 25 minutes; spray with oil and bake a further 10 minutes, until golden.

14. Pour cream over rolls if desired.

FRUITSOURCE® is infintely preferable to regular sugar for three reasons:

1) It has nutrients.

2) Because it is made of grape juice and grains, it is only partially a simple sugar and therefore does not give a sugar buzz.

3) It provides sweetness without being obvious, allowing the real flavors of the recipes to shine.

FruitSource® comes in sugar and syrup forms, and is available in health food stores or the health food sections of grocery stores (or call 408-457-1136, or write to Customer Service, 445 Vick Drive, Santa Cruz, CA 95060).

CHAPTER TEN

Just Desserts

CREAM AND ICE CREAM

There are a number of creams on the market but none of them deliver the rich, complex, creamy, and yet light nectar that this one does (while using no dairy products and having no cholesterol). As an ice cream, it is on a par with the creamy HDs that we all so love to slurp. Use sparingly, though—it has nut fats and calories in plenty—about 7 grams of fat per ¹/₂ cup; but that is still less than half of those addictive HDs.

Makes 3 cups
15 minutes

1	*cup almonds, blanched*
1	*cup cashews, blanched*
¹/₂	*cup coconut milk*
1 ¹/₂	*cups amasake (or almond, soy or rice milk)*
³/₄	*cup maple syrup*
1	*tablespoon vanilla*
¹/₈	*teaspoon salt*
¹/₄	*cup dry sherry*
2	*teaspoons agar flakes*

1. Food process almonds and cashews 1 minute until a powder.
2. Add coconut milk, 1 cup amasake, syrup, vanilla, salt and sherry and process 2 minutes.
3. Combine remaining amasake with agar in a small pot, bring to boil and simmer 5 minutes.
4. Strain almond/cashew mix through a very fine sieve and do the same for the agar mix to remove any undissolved solids.
5. Combine all ingredients in the processor and blend 2 minutes.

6. Refrigerate (or freeze for ice cream).

You can use any nuts to make a cream or ice cream. Just substitute the chosen nuts in place of the almonds and cashews. You might want to try a different liqueur, such as Kahlua for hazelnuts/filberts. And if using filberts, the bitter inner skins need to be removed (bake at 350° for 6 minutes and place on a towel to rub them off).

Make a dessert out of the remaining nut meals by topping off with some of the cream and garnishing with a few toasted nuts.

AGAR is an effective and easy-to-use gelatin derived from sea plants. It is preferred to the gelatin we normally buy, which is made of the joints and hooves of animals. Agar only requires 1 tablesoon to thicken a quart of liquid and is high in minerals.

AMASAKE is thicker than any other milks (dairy and non-dairy). It is a fermented, rice-based drink. Both agar and amasake can be purchased in health food stores.

ALMOND FLAN

A traditional Mexican desert.

Serves 8
30 minutes plus 30 minutes refrigeration

$1/2$	cup maple syrup
1	quart almond milk (or amasake, soy or rice milks)
1	tablespoon arrowroot
$1/2$	cup FruitSource® sugar
$1/4$	cup agar flakes
1	teaspoon vanilla
1	teaspoon almond essence
2	teaspoons allspice
1	cup almond cream (pg 153)
	Pinch salt
2	tablespoons orange juice
$1/2$	cup raspberry jelly
$1/4$	cup almonds, chopped

1. Heat maple syrup and simmer 20 minutes until thickened slightly.

2. Dissolve arrowroot in $1/4$ cup milk; stir in sugar and let sit 5 minutes.

3. Dissolve agar in remaining milk, bring to boil and simmer while stirring until agar has almost dissolved, about 5 minutes. Strain through sieve.

4. In same pot, combine arrowroot mix, spices, cream and salt; simmer while stirring for 5 minutes until thickens, then let cool.

5. Spoon thickened maple syrup into each of eight 2 $1/2$-inch ramekins, smear on bottoms and sides with a finger and refrigerate to harden.

6. Pour flan mix into ramekins and refrigerate.

7. Mix juice and jelly into a sauce, pour over puddings and sprinkle with chopped almonds.

ARROWROOT is preferred to cornstarch in puddings as it is easier to digest, doesn't require a high temperature to lose that starchy taste, and leaves the food translucent.

It should be dissolved in cold water before being introduced to hot water to prevent lumping.

KUZU is very similar and can be substituted exactly for arrowroot. It has the added advantage of being useable as a glaze on desserts and puddings. It can generally only be found in health food stores, whereas supermarkets carry arrowroot.

APPLE CRUMBLE

While "As American as Apple Pie" is almost axiomatic in America, it is also a tribute to the pervasive influence of the British, who have enjoyed apple pie and apple crumble for the last 500 years. The difference between pies and crumbles is mainly in the crusts. In England, a crumble is usually eaten with hot custard, rather than the ice cream that Americans enjoy.

Serves 6
30 minutes plus 30 minutes baking

Filling

$^1/_2$	cup orange juice, freshly squeezed
1	tablespoon arrowroot
$^1/_2$	cup raspberry jelly
$^1/_3$	cup FruitSource® sugar
$^1/_2$	teaspoon cinnamon
$^1/_8$	teaspoon nutmeg
$^1/_2$	cup raisins
2	tablespoons lemon juice
7	cups Granny Smith apples

Crumble

1 ½ *cups whole wheat pastry flour*
1   *cup rolled oats, ground*
1   *teaspoon cinnamon*
¼   *teaspoon nutmeg*
⅛   *teaspoon ginger*
½   *teaspoon sea salt*
¼   *cup almonds or cashews, chopped*
¼   *cup maple syrup*
1   *banana, mashed*
1   *cup cream (pg 153)*

1. In a medium bowl, dissolve arrowroot into juice, blend in jelly and then stir in sugar, spices, and raisins and set aside.

2. Peel, core and thinly slice apples and place in a large bowl with lemon juice and set aside.

3. Preheat oven to 375° F.

4. Combine dry crumble ingredients and add nuts.

5. Mix syrup, banana and ¼ cup cream.

6. Add the liquid to the flour mix and work until uniformly crumb-like.

7. Combine raisin mix with apples.

8. Transfer filling to six 4-inch ramekins, or a small casserole dish.

9. Sprinkle crumble over filling.

10. Bake about 30 minutes until apples are soft and crust crunchy.

11. Serve hot or warm, with remaining cream or ice cream.

Did you ever notice that the cashew nuts sold in stores never have shells around them? The reason is that the cashew nut is related to poison ivy and the shells harbor some of the same irritants.

PEACH COBBLER

Serves 6
20 minutes plus one hour baking

²/₃   cup (amasake) milk
2   teaspoons canola oil
2   teaspoons raspberry vinegar
¹/₂   cup FruitSource® or maple syrup
6   tablespoons arrowroot
1   cup whole wheat pastry flour
¹/₂   cup unbleached flour
⁵/₈   teaspoon salt
1   cup fresh fruit juice
1 ¹/₂ teaspoons and one pinch cinnamon
¹/₂   teaspoon nutmeg
2 ¹/₂ quarts fresh or frozen peaches, peeled, pitted and sliced

1. In a mixing bowl, whisk amasake, oil, vinegar, and 1 table-spoon each of syrup and arrowroot.
2. Mix flours and ¹/₂ teaspoon salt; pour liquid mix into flour and work to form dough into a ball; roll into a circle shape, approximately ¹/₈" thick. Set aside.
3. Preheat oven to 425°.
4. In a 10-inch, deep baking dish, combine juice, spices, remaining arrowroot and salt, and ¹/₂ cup of syrup. Place peaches in mix.
5. Cover with pastry and make a few vents. Mix remaining syrup with pinch cinnamon and brush over crust.
6. Bake 15 minutes and lower to 375° another 45 minutes until crust lightly browned. Cover cobbler loosely with foil to prevent burning if needed, removing last 15 minutes.
7. Serve hot or cold.

Variation

This recipe works well with any fruit.

CHOCOLATE CAKE

The word "Cacao" is Aztec for the tree and seeds that produce chocolate. The word "chocolate" itself is also Aztec for the product of these seeds. The Aztecs and Mayans considered chocolate to be an aphrodisiac. This wishful thought was not lost on the Europeans who took cocoa back home four centuries ago, as the whole of Europe ended up with the same idea. Maybe Madison Avenue wasn't the first after all to lure customers with sexy images to sell consumer products. Today, chocolate still seems to seduce our appetites and hopefully the recipes that follow will be no different.

Serves 16
15 minutes and 45 minutes baking

$1/2$ *cup amasake or soy milk*
2   *cups FruitSource® sugar*
$1/2$ *cup hazelnut or canola oil*
1   *ripe banana*
1   *teaspoon vanilla*
1   *cup hazelnut cream (pg 153)*
1   *teaspoon baking soda*
$2/3$ *cup cocoa or carob powder*
$1/2$ *teaspoon salt*
1 $1/2$ *cups whole wheat pastry flour*
1   *cup unbleached flour*
     Canola oil spray
1   *punnet (small basket) of raspberries*

1. Pre-heat oven to 350°.
2. In a mixer or blender, mix sugar with milk and let sit 5 minutes.
3. Blend in oil, banana, vanilla and cream.
4. Mix dry ingredients in a bowl, and add to rest of ingredients, blending well.
5. Grease two eight-inch, round baking tins/dishes and pour cake mix into them.
6. Bake 45 minutes until a knife inserted in the middle comes out clean, and the edges of the cakes separate from the edge of the tin.

7. Once cooled, spread frosting over the top of one cake; place the other cake on top of the first, and then cover its top and their combined sides with frosting.

8. Garnish with fresh raspberries.

CHOCOLATE FROSTING

5 minutes

³/₄ cup cocoa or carob powder
1   cup FruitSource® sugar
1   tablespoon hazelnut or canola oil
¹/₄ cup Kahlua
1   cup (hazelnut) cream (pg 153)

1. Blend ingredients until smooth.
2. Spread over cake.

In the great chocolate v's carob debate, chocolate has the advantage on smoothness and flavor, although carob becomes passably smooth when heated gently or combined with a hot liquid. Carob, on the other hand, has the health advantage on four counts: it contains 1% of the fat found in chocolate; it does not require insulin to break it down, making it acceptable to diabetics. It has natural sugars in it, unlike chocolate, and so requires less added sugars which reduces the likelihood of cavities. And lastly, carob does not create allergic reactions (unlike chocolate for some). So you decide which you'd rather use in these recipes.

SOUR CHERRY CHOCOLATE TORTE

Serves 20 (thin wedges as so rich)
40 minutes plus 1 hour baking

1	cup kirsch liqueur
¹/₂	pound dry pitted cherries
2	tablespoons canola oil
1	teaspoon arrowroot
2	cups (amasake or soy) milk
2	cups cocoa or carob powder
1 ²/₃	cups (soy) milk
¹/₂	cup maple syrup, canola or liquid FruitSource®
3	teaspoons vanilla
¹/₄	teaspoon almond essence
¹/₂	cup almonds, blanched and finely ground
1	ripe banana, mashed
²/₃	cup powdered FruitSource® or succanat
²/₃	cup whole wheat pastry flour
¹/₂	cup almond cream (pg 153)

1. Combine kirsch and cherries in saucepan, bring to boil and let stand off heat half an hour to plump cherries.

2. Grease a 9-inch spring-form pan with 1 tablespoon canola and dust with 1 tablespoon cocoa powder.

3. Heat milk; place cocoa and arrowroot in a processor and mix briefly. To processor, add warmed milk, remaining oil, maple syrup, vanilla, almond essence, almonds, banana, powdered sweetener, flour and blend.

4. Pre-heat oven to 350°.

5. Spread half the mix into pan; place cherries in single layer on top; spoon rest of mix onto cherries.

6. Bake in lower third of oven 60 minutes until a cake tester proves clean. Cover loosely with foil if top darkens prematurely. Cool in pan on a rack.

7. Mix almond cream with remains of the kirsch soaking liquid and refrigerate until ready to serve with torte.

BANANA CREAM PIE

Serves 12
15 minutes plus 10 minutes baking

2 *tablespoons canola oil*
1 *5-oz box honey grahams*
1 *cup macadamia nuts*
3 *ripe bananas*
   Juice of half a lemon
4 *cups cream (pg 153)*
2 *tablespoons coconut, shredded*
10 *raspberries*

1. Preheat oven to 375°.
2. Blend half oil, honey grahams and macadamia nuts into meal.
3. Press into a 9-inch pie plate.
4. Bake 10 minutes until golden.
5. Slice bananas and coat in lemon juice.
6. Place ½ bananas on crust, pour cream on top and layer rest of bananas on top. Sprinkle with coconut and freeze.
7. Refrigerate 30 minutes before serving, and garnish with raspberries.

ALASKAN CHOCOLATE MOOSE PIE

One of those interminably dark, Alaskan winter days inspired this triumph over cabin fever.

Serves 10
20 minutes

1	*5-oz box honey grahams*
1	*cup macadamia nuts*
2	*tablespoons canola (or hazelnut) oil*
1	*tablespoon kuzu*
⅓	*cup maple syrup*
30	*oz soft tofu*
1	*tablespoon vanilla*
1	*teaspoon lemon rind, minced*
½	*cup cocoa or carob powder*
½	*cup cream (pg 153)*

1. Preheat oven to 375°.
2. Food process honey grahams and macadamia nuts into meal (add oil if lower fat-content nuts are used).
3. Press into a 9-inch pie plate.
4. Bake 10 minutes until golden. Cool in refrigerator.
5. Combine syrup and kuzu, bring to simmer and stir until dissolved.
6. Blend tofu, vanilla, lemon rind, maple syrup mix until smooth.
7. Remove half and set aside.
8. Add cocoa or carob to remaining mix and blend 5 minutes.
9. Pour both mixes onto crust and mix slightly with knife to create patterns.
10. Refrigerate.
11. Serve with cream.

KEY LIME PIE

Serves 12
25 minutes plus 1 hour cooling and chilling

1   *tablespoons canola oil*
1   *5-oz box honey grahams*
1   *cup macadamia nuts*
¼   *cup arrowroot*
¾   *cup (key) lime juice*
¼   *cup (amasake) milk*
3   *cups macadamia cream (pg 153)*
3   *oz soft tofu*
3   *tablespoons grated lime rind*
¼   *cup macadamia nuts, coarsely chopped*
2   *kiwis, peeled and sliced*

1. Pre-heat oven to 375°.

2. Food process oil, crackers and nuts into meal, and press into 9-inch pie plate.

3. Bake 15 minutes until golden and cool in fridge.

4. Add arrowroot to lime juice and milk and bring to simmer, stirring constantly.

5. Thoroughly blend arrowroot mix, cream, tofu and rind.

6. Pour mix into pie shell and top with nuts and kiwi.

7. Freeze.

8. Refrigerate two hours before serving.

The only difference you will notice between the next two pies and the ones usually eaten at Thanksgiving and Christmas is that you won't feel heavy and sugared-out after eating them.

PECAN PIE

Serves 8
55 minutes

Crust

²/₃ cup (amasake) milk
2   teaspoons canola oil
2   teaspoons raspberry vinegar
1   tablespoon FruitSource® or maple syrup
1   tablespoon arrowroot
1   cup whole wheat pastry flour
¹/₂ cup unbleached flour
¹/₂ teaspoon salt

Filling

1   cup pecans, crushed
1   cup pecans, halved
2   cups (amasake) milk
¹/₂ cup FruitSource® sugar
1   cup maple syrup
¹/₄ teaspoon salt
¹/₂ lemon rind, grated
3   tablespoons canola oil
1   teaspoon vanilla
4   tablespoons agar flakes
3   tablespoons arrowroot
1   cup pecan cream (pg 153)

1. Preheat oven to 300° F.
2. In a mixing bowl, whisk amasake, oil, vinegar, syrup and arrowroot.

3. Mix flour and salt; pour liquid mix into flour and work to form dough into a ball; roll into a circle shape, approximately $^1/_8$" thick and place in a pie pan.

4. Bake 40 minutes and let cool.

5. In the same oven, roast pecans for 20 minutes until fragrant.

6. In a large saucepan, combine milk and sugar and let sit 5 minutes. Add remaining ingredients (except cream) to pan, whisk together; bring to boil and simmer 5 minutes until agar dissolved.

7. Layer crushed nuts on bottom of crust.

8. Pour in custard mixture.

9. Lay halved pecans on top of custard mix.

10. Serve with pecan cream.

PUMPKIN PIE

Make this a day ahead for improved flavor.

Serves 8
20 minutes and 1 - 2 hours baking

Crust

2/3   cup (amasake) milk
2   teaspoons canola oil
2   teaspoons raspberry vinegar
1   tablespoon FruitSource® or maple syrup
1   tablespoon arrowroot
1   cup whole wheat pastry flour
1/2   cup unbleached flour
1/2   teaspoon salt

Filling

1   small pumpkin (or 16-oz can pumpkin)
1   cup soft tofu
3/4   cup FruitSource® or maple syrup
1/2   teaspoon salt
2   teaspoons cinnamon
1/2   teaspoon ginger
1/2   teaspoon cloves
1/2   teaspoon nutmeg
1   teaspoon vanilla
2   cups cream (pg 153)

1. Preheat oven to 300° F.
2. In a mixing bowl, whisk amasake, oil, vinegar, syrup and arrowroot.
3. Mix flour and 1/2 teaspoon salt; pour liquid mix into flour and work to form dough into a ball; roll into a circle shape, approximately 1/8" thick.
4. Bake 15 minutes and let cool.
5. Either open the can, or preheat oven to 375°, halve and deseed pumpkin, bake cut side down for 1 hour, until a fork pierces it easily. Reduce oven to 350°. Scoop out flesh.
6. In blender, combine 2 cups pumpkin, tofu, syrup, salt, spices, 1 cup cream and puree.
7. Pour into pie shell and bake 45 minutes.
8. Serve with remaining cream.

CREPES SUZETTE

Serves 4
20 minutes and 1 hour allowing mix to stand

½   cup whole wheat flour
½   cup unbleached flour
1   cup (amasake or soy) milk
1   teaspoon arrowroot
¼   teaspoon salt
¼   teaspoon nutmeg
1   tablespoon apple juice or cognac
4   ripe bananas, diced
4   tablespoons canola oil
4   tablespoons maple syrup
6   tablespoons marmalade
1   tablespoon cointreau
2   tablespoons orange juice, fresh

1. Heat flour in dry skillet over medium until golden and fragrant.
2. Whisk flours, milk, arrowroot, salt, nutmeg and apple juice.
3. Let stand one hour at room temperature.
4. Meanwhile, fry bananas in half the oil and syrup, about 2 minutes.
5. Stir marmalade, cointreau and lemon juice into banana mix.
6. With 1 teaspoon oil heated in a small skillet on medium heat, pour enough batter to thinly cover skillet and fry till golden, 1 – 2 minutes each side.
7. Place mix on the dough and roll into cigar shapes.
8. Sprinkle with remaining maple syrup and broil 1 – 2 minutes.

ANOTHER FUDGE BROWNIE

The Brownie is the quintessential American treat: rich and easy to make. Created in the 1920's, it became popular during the World War II when mothers joined the work force and had less time to cook. The circumstances haven't changed really, but this recipe takes the sinfulness out of the indulgence while giving it a new twist.

Serves 8
15 minutes

1/2	cup plumped raisins
1	teaspoon vanilla
1/4	teaspoon almond essence
2	tablespoons coffee liqueur
3/4	cup (amasake or soy) milk
1	cup FruitSource® sugar
1	tablespoons canola oil
1	tablespoon instant decaf coffee (optional)
6	tablespoons cocoa or carob powder
1 1/4	cups whole wheat flour
1/2	teaspoon baking powder
3/4	teaspoon salt
1	cup pecans, chopped
1/2	cup FruitSource®-sweetened chocolate or carob chips
1	teaspoon orange peel, grated
	Butter spray

1. Combine raisins, vanilla, almond and liqueur and let sit.
2. Combine sugar in a mixing bowl with milk and let sit 5 minutes. Add oil, coffee and cocoa/carob and blend until smooth.
3. Pre-heat oven to 350°.
4. Combine flour, baking powder and salt.
5. Blend chocolate mix into flour.
6. Mix in remaining ingredients.
7. Spray an 8x8x2 baking pan, pour in mix and bake 40 minutes until a knife inserted in the center proves clean.

OATMEAL CHOCOLATE CHIP COOKIES

Cookies apparently originated in Persia (Iran) 1,300 years ago. We don't know their recipes, but they certainly did not have chocolate chips in them, like half of all home-made cookies in America today. This version is the result of European, American and vegetarian culinary influences. While it may not be the same as the oatmeal chocolate chip cookies you are used to, we beg your indulgence, that you may decide on the merits of the cookie without prejudice. In other words, give it a go, it's a great new taste and texture.

Makes 2 dozen cookies
20 minutes plus 25 minutes baking

$^1/_2$	cup sherry
$^1/_2$	cup raisins and/or dried cranberries
1 $^1/_2$	cups (amasake or soy) milk
1	teaspoon vanilla
1 $^1/_4$	cups FruitSource® sugar
1	tablespoon safflower or canola oil
2	teaspoons baking soda, dissolved in 1 teaspoon hot water
1 $^1/_2$	cups whole wheat pastry flour
3	cups rolled oats or granola, coarsely ground
1	teaspoon salt
$^1/_4$	teaspoon nutmeg
1	teaspoon cinnamon
1	cup FruitSource®-sweetened chocolate or carob chips
1	cup pecans, chopped
1	tablespoon orange rind, freshly grated

1. Preheat oven to 375°.
2. In small pan, heat sherry and plump raisins for 10 minutes.
3. In medium bowl, mix vanilla into and add sugar. Let sit 5 minutes, stirring occasionally.
4. Add oil and soda to milk mix.
5. In another bowl, mix flour, oats, salt and spices.
6. Add liquid to dry ingredients and mix.
7. Stir in chips, pecans, raisins, sherry and rind.
8. Place heaping tablespoon dough on parchment-covered

cookie sheets, flatten to a circular $1/4$-inch thick and bake until golden and cookie returns to its shape after being gently pressed with a finger, 15 minutes. Switch off oven.

9. Let cookies cool on a wire tray for 10 minutes, turn over and return to cooling oven for 10 minutes.

They will be crispy when cooled.

Variation

For a richer treat, substitute pecan cream (pg 153) for milk.

Have you ever wondered when to use baking powder and when to use baking soda? Baking powder is baking soda with cream of tartar added. They both provide lightness to cake and bread mixes, but baking soda results in the lightest textures and is preferred in recipes which have some acidic ingredient.

PEANUT BUTTER COOKIES

Makes 2 dozen cookies
15 minutes plus 30 minutes chilling/baking

2	*teaspoons vanilla*
1/4	*cup (amasake) milk*
1	*cup FruitSource® sugar*
1	*tablespoon canola oil*
1	*cup chunky peanut butter, unsweetened, unsalted*
1 1/4	*cups whole wheat pastry flour*
1/2	*teaspoon baking powder*
3/4	*teaspoon baking soda*
1/4	*teaspoon salt*

1. Add vanilla to milk in a bowl and then add sugar and let sit 5 minutes, stirring occasionally.
2. Mix oil and peanut butter and add to sugar mix.
3. Combine rest of ingredients in a larger bowl.
4. Mix liquid ingredients into flour mix.
5. Chill dough.
6. Preheat oven to 375°.
7. Roll into large walnut sized balls.
8. Place cookies on parchment covered cookie sheet.
9. Dip fork in flour and imprint lattice patterns on each cookie.
10. Bake till light finger pressure rebounds, 10 – 15 minutes (even 18 minutes, if dough very chilled).

Variation

Substitute almond or cashew nuts.

Epilogue

You have been exposed no doubt over the years to a barrage of information and misinformation about the poor health of the different environments on this planet. Although we have concerned ourselves in this book with your own personal health, we would like to offer a new angle on the relationship between your eating habits and environment.

For centuries, man has been surviving on one diet or another, whether predominantly vegetarian, meat- or fish-eating. He has accomplished this by fishing the seas, hunting or raising lower life forms or cultivating plants and trees. These solutions have all worked to one degree or another at different times and in different places. This fact does not mean that these are necessarily the best ways for us to continue feeding ourselves today. The acknowledged history of planet Earth has never included multi-billions of inhabitants all needing to eat. The old solutions for feeding this many people have resulted in the loss of fertile soil, fish stocks disappearing from the oceans, birds and other natural pest-control agents drastically reduced in numbers, a loss of diversity of crops, the disappearance of game as a source of food, contribution to apparent global warming and pollution of the land, seas and rivers of the world.

It is clear that the environment will increasingly fail to provide the food we need to survive. It may seem unlikely, surrounded as we are by grocery stores full of packaged foods and fields of wheat, but behind the scenes, the situation for our children, or their children at least, is not so rosey.

As an individual, you can do something about the global situation as well as your own environment. Eating a vegetarian meal just once a week is a good start. You may wonder how that can possibly effect all the problems listed above. Well, let's take one person, sitting alone at a large dining table, eating his or her way through a one pound steak. Now let's imagine that person sharing the table with fifteen other people, all enjoying a vegetarian meal which took the same amount of farmland and environmental resources to produce as that one pound of steak. The power of the table fork is not to be underestimated, nor the power of the person wielding it, and we hope you will exercise your options.

GLOSSARY

Agar A tasteless sea vegetable used as a gelling agent.

Amasake Fermented and sweet beverage made from rice.

Arrowroot A better alternative to cornstarch made from the root of a tropical plant and used for thickening.

Balsamic Vinegar A semi-sweet vinegar made from white grapes but red-brown in color.

Bok Choy Chinese White Cabbage.

Bragg Liquid Aminos Non-fermented soy-sauce alternative.

Canola Oil Tasteless oil made from rapeseed, lowest of all oils in saturated fats.

Carob Low in fat and non-addictive, carob is similar to chocolate.

Cilantro Also known as coriander or Chinese parsely.

FruitSource® Brand name for a sweetener made of grapes and rice.

Gluten A protein found in wheat used to make "wheat meat."

Kombu A dried sea vegetable used in beans, soups, and stews in place of salt.

Kuzu/Kudzu White chunks of tasteless root starch used as thickener.

Mirin Low alchohol, Japanese cooking wine made from rice.

Miso A wine-flavored, fermented paste used as a salt substitute.

Nayonaise® Brand name for mayonaise made from soy beans and without eggs.

Pesto A pasta sauce usually made of olive oil, basil, pine nuts and Parmesan.

Pine nuts   Pignoli—edible seeds of some pine trees.

Portobello   Meaty and flavorful mushrooms with very large caps
Mushrooms

Seitan   A bland wheat gluten, high in protein.

Shiitake   Large-capped, dark, and flavorful mushrooms, available dried or fresh.

Silken tofu   Custard-like bean curd available in soft, firm, and extra firm textures.

Soy milk   Milk made from ground and boiled soy beans.

Soy sauce   A flavor enhancer made of salt, water, wheat, and fermented beans.

Tamari   Soy sauce made without wheat.

Tempeh   Fermented and cooked soy beans, often made with grains such as millet.

Tofu   Bean curd.

TVP   Textured Vegetable Protein made into chunks, strips, or granules from de-fatted soy flour.

Vegan   Person who eats only fruit, vegetables, grains, legumes, and nuts, or the diet itself.

Vegetarian   As with Vegan, but including dairy products and eggs.

ABOUT JAIN PUBLISHING COMPANY

Jain Publishing Company is a diversified publisher of books and related products covering subject areas such as business/management, computers/internet, health/healing, motivation/inspiration, self-help/psychology, personal finance and religions/philosophies. We also publish fine gift books and occasional vegetarian cookbooks. Additionally, under our imprint, **Asian Humanities Press**, we publish scholarly as well as general interest books in the subjects of Asian religions/philosophies and languages/literature. Many of our books under both imprints are used as college textbooks as well. A complete, up to date listing of all our products, with color illustrations, descriptions, review excerpts, specifications and prices is always available on-line at our web site at the following address:

http://www.jainpub.com

We invite you to browse through our on-line catalog from time to time to find out what is available and what is forthcoming. We also encourage you to communicate your comments and suggestions to us via e-mail. Our e-mail address is mail@jainpub.com.